THE CHRONICLES
OF THE
JEWISH
PEOPLE

THE CHRONICLES
OF THE
JEWISH
PEOPLE

Raymond P. Scheindlin

SMITHMARK

ACKNOWLEDGMENTS

I would like to thank Professor Mark Cohen for his friendship and encouragement, for his careful reading of the manuscript, and for his many suggestions for its improvement. Thanks are also due to Tony Burgess and Hallie Einhorn for their excellent editorial work; to Wendy Missan and Barbara Gold for their painstaking selection of the artwork; and to my loyal and good-natured research assistant, Nina Nesher. My wife, Janice Meyerson, contributed to this project, as she does to all my projects, her acute reading skills and astute editorial advice, both administered with her distinctive combination of wit and whimsy.

A FRIEDMAN GROUP BOOK

This edition published in 1996 by SMITHMARK Publishers, a division of U.S. Media Holdings, Inc., 16 East 32nd Street, New York, NY 10016

SMITHMARK book are available for bulk purchase for sales promotion and premium use. For details write or call the manager of special sales, SMITHMARK Publlishers, 16 East 32nd Street, New York, NY; (212) 532-6600

ISBN 1-0-7651-9975-0

CHRONICLES OF THE JEWISH PEOPLE
was prepared and produced by
Michael Friedman Publishing Group, Inc.
15 West 26th Street
New York, NY 10010

Editor: Tony Burgess
Art Director: Lynne Yeamans
Designer: Barbara Gold
Photography Editor: Wendy Missan

Color separation by Ocean Graphic International Company Ltd.
Printed in China by Leefung-Asco Printers Ltd.

THE CHRONICLES
OF THE
JEWISH
PEOPLE

Raymond P. Scheindlin

SMITHMARK

ACKNOWLEDGMENTS

I would like to thank Professor Mark Cohen for his friendship and encouragement, for his careful reading of the manuscript, and for his many suggestions for its improvement. Thanks are also due to Tony Burgess and Hallie Einhorn for their excellent editorial work; to Wendy Missan and Barbara Gold for their painstaking selection of the artwork; and to my loyal and good-natured research assistant, Nina Nesher. My wife, Janice Meyerson, contributed to this project, as she does to all my projects, her acute reading skills and astute editorial advice, both administered with her distinctive combination of wit and whimsy.

A FRIEDMAN GROUP BOOK

This edition published in 1996 by SMITHMARK Publishers, a division of U.S. Media Holdings, Inc., 16 East 32nd Street, New York, NY 10016

SMITHMARK book are available for bulk purchase for sales promotion and premium use. For details write or call the manager of special sales, SMITHMARK Publlishers, 16 East 32nd Street, New York, NY; (212) 532-6600

ISBN 1-0-7651-9975-0

CHRONICLES OF THE JEWISH PEOPLE
was prepared and produced by
Michael Friedman Publishing Group, Inc.
15 West 26th Street
New York, NY 10010

Editor: Tony Burgess
Art Director: Lynne Yeamans
Designer: Barbara Gold
Photography Editor: Wendy Missan

Color separation by Ocean Graphic International Company Ltd.
Printed in China by Leefung-Asco Printers Ltd.

CONTENTS

INTRODUCTION

WHO ARE THE JEWS?

Millions of people worldwide think of themselves as Jews or are thought of as Jews by others; but these widely scattered millions differ in physical type, language, dress, customs, folkways, and citizenship. And despite the existence of a Jewish religion, the Jews are not united by any one system of belief; rather, the Jewish people is made up of individuals who embrace many different religious outlooks besides traditional Judaism, as well as free-thinkers, atheists, and the religiously indifferent. So what makes a person a Jew?

The only reliable answer is provided by history. The Jews are a people that once formed a nation with its own land, language, and culture; despite the loss—millennia ago—of these features of nationhood, the descendants of this people have retained their sense of national identity, common history, and, in part, common destiny. Their very antiquity is part of their identity; among the peoples of the Western world, they are the only surviving group that existed as a nation before the Romans. Survivors from a time before Western civilization took shape, they have taken on the coloration of the nations and cultures among whom they were scattered. Their culture is as varied as the cultures among which they have lived; but their identity and their unity reside in the consciousness of their common origins and shared experiences.

To know the Jews' history, we have to know the history of the peoples that have been their hosts over the centuries. The Chronicles of the Jewish People is the story of how the Jews have experienced world history; it is a fabric woven with pictures of many cultures of the Eastern and Western worlds, with one historic group—the Jews—as a common thread.

Thus, in discussing medieval Jewry, we will not understand the creativity and openness of the Jews in the Islamic world without understanding the extent to which that world dominated Western culture during the period. The achievements of Maimonides can be made clear only when due attention is given to his Arabic and Islamic environment, while the attempt to describe him solely as a product of internal Jewish developments would lead only to a flat, idealized, and unrealistic picture. Likewise, the advent of Zionism, the creation of the State of Israel, and the revival of Hebrew as a spoken language can only be explained in the context of nineteenth-century European nationalist movements. The same principle holds true for the entire history of the Jewish Diaspora.

The Chronicles of the Jewish People *covers the entire sweep of the Jewish experience from legendary times to the peace agreements now being negotiated in the Middle East. Each chapter covers one of the chronological units generally accepted among historians (for example, Chapter One: The Israelite Kingdom; Chapter Two: The Second Jewish State). For most periods, simultaneous chronological units are divided up between two chapters, permitting different cultural spheres to be accorded separate treatment (for example, Chapter Four: The Jews in the Islamic World, Part I (622–1500); Chapter Five: The Jews of Medieval Christendom).*

At the end of The Chronicles of the Jewish People *the reader will find a chronology in the form of a double time line; one line represents the major events of Jewish history, and the other, the major events of world history. In addition, each chapter contains a number of side-bars profiling important people or highlighting noteworthy facts distinctive to the period or culture that is the subject of the chapter.*

It may seem audacious to attempt to present the history of the Jews in such a short compass. Executing the plan necessitated difficult decisions about what to omit and how to compress what was retained. But such a brief presentation has a distinct advantage: it permits readers to survey the entire history of the Jews quickly—in one or two sittings—so that they can easily grasp the long lines of continuity. With this broad perspective, they will more easily come to grasp why the Jews, for all their variety, sense themselves to be united by a single destiny. And if, in the course of reading, readers find any particular period or theme to be especially interesting, they can always follow it up, thanks to the enormous volume of literature that has been produced over the years by historians of the Jews.

CHAPTER ONE

THE ISRAELITE KINGDOM

*T*he earliest origins of the Jewish people are buried in legends so vivid that they obscure the actual facts. The oldest narrative is the Book of Genesis, but it was written much later than the events it describes; and none of the ancient Near Eastern writings mentions the earliest Israelites.

Yet the general outline of the story in Genesis agrees with what we know of the history of the land of Israel in the second millennium B.C., a history of east-west migration from Mesopotamia (present-day Iraq) to the land of Canaan (roughly equivalent to present-day Israel, Jordan, Lebanon, and part of Syria). These migrants were called West Semites or Amorites, and their language came to be known as Canaanite. They established small principalities along the plains and coastal areas that were under the control of Egypt. New groups kept coming and either joined those already established or moved on to new territories. By the nineteenth century B.C., the first waves of migrants had arrived in Egypt proper. At the same time, new groups—Indo-Europeans and Hurrians—began to invade the land of Canaan. Some of these migrants also reached Egypt, where, together with the West Semitic nomads, they formed a mixed group called the Hyksos. The Hyksos actually succeeded in taking control of Egypt from 1655 to 1570 B.C., at which point they were driven out of that land.

These movements correspond roughly with the stories of the Bible. According to Genesis, Abraham was a nomad from Mesopotamia who left at God's bidding for Canaan, where he and his descendants—

TOP: Clay tablet with cuneiform inscription found at Hazor, Israel. The tablet records a lawsuit from some time between the eighteenth and the sixteenth centuries B.C.

BOTTOM: Semitic nomads arriving in Egypt bearing gifts for a governor's tomb, as depicted in an ancient Egyptian wall painting.

Isaac, Jacob, and their children—lived on the margin of the established settlements, raising cattle, sheep, and goats, and occasionally farming. They generally avoided mingling with the majority population, though conflicts sometimes occurred. Viewed by the local populace as resident aliens, they were grouped with a larger, mixed class of marginal peoples that could be found interspersed among the established population. This class was called *Ḥabiru*, and the name eventually was attached to the descendants of Abraham in the form "Hebrew," especially after they came to Egypt as part of the Hyksos.

The Bible does not describe these large migratory movements, but focuses on the family of Jacob, relating that they were driven to Egypt by famine, and that one of Jacob's younger sons, Joseph, became a powerful courtier there. According to the story, when the pharaoh who had favored Joseph died, a new pharaoh came to power who oppressed the Israelites, as the descendants of Jacob were called. This development would correspond to the

ABOVE: According to the Bible, God tested Abraham's loyalty by ordering him to offer his son Isaac as a sacrifice on Mount Moriah. In this painting by James J. Tissot (1836–1902), Isaac carries the wood and Abraham carries coals for the fire.

RIGHT: Isaac and his brother Ishmael burying their father, Abraham, as depicted in a fourteenth-century Latin Bible manuscript. According to tradition, Isaac was the ancestor of the Jews and Ishmael of the Arabs.

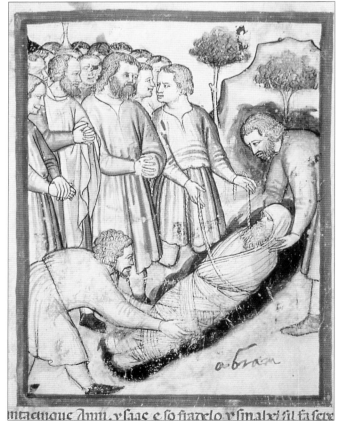

LEFT: *Jacob's Dream*, by Raphael (1483–1520). Jacob, the third patriarch of Israel, fled his brother Esau to Mesopotamia. On the way, he dreamt of a ladder with angels going up and down it and God at the top, proclaiming that he would one day return to Canaan and possess it.

BELOW: A diorama depicting the construction of the pyramid of King Mycerinus in the twenty-sixth century B.C. at Giza in Egypt. Although this construction took place about a thousand years before the enslavement of the Israelites as described in the Bible, the diorama allows one to imagine the Israelite slaves at their forced labor.

BOTTOM: The great sphinx and the pyramids at Giza.

end of the Hyksos' power and their expulsion from Egypt, when it would be natural for the Egyptians to enslave the remaining Semites. The Bible says that the Israelite slaves were forced to build two Egyptian cities, which are known by archaeological evidence to have been built during the reign of Ramses II (1304–1237 B.C.). The Bible also says that the Israelites fled Egypt under the reign of the next pharaoh, presumably Ramses' successor Merneptah. An Egyptian inscription dated 1220 B.C. that has survived from the reign of Merneptah mentions Israel in connection with Merneptah's battles in Palestine. This is the first reference to ancient Israel in a contemporaneous source.

The later Jewish tradition, as recorded in the Bible, would look back at these events in ancient Egypt as part of a divine plan for God's chosen people. According to the biblical account, Abraham had left Mesopotamia with God's promise to guide him and to bring him and his descendants prosperity. Upon Abraham's reaching Canaan, God informed him that his descendants would be enslaved in Egypt, but that they would eventually return to Canaan and live there under His protection forever. Jacob's sons sold their hated brother Joseph into slavery, not realizing that their action was part of a divine plan to bring Joseph to Egypt in advance of their own forced migration there. By the time they arrived, Joseph had gained enough power that he was able to provide for them, establishing them in the land of Goshen, in the Nile delta.

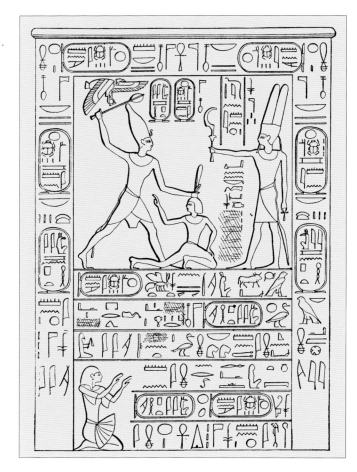

ABOVE: Egyptian hieroglyphic inscription of Pharaoh Merneptah (r. 1236–23 B.C.), the presumed Pharaoh of the Exodus. He is depicted here triumphing over foreign enemies, including the Israelites. This is the first reference to Israel in an inscription.

BELOW: The Exodus, by Marc Chagall (1887–1985). Moses is depicted with attributes of Christ in the center; at the lower right corner he is depicted again as lawgiver.

According to the Bible, the enslaved Israelites were led out of Egypt by Moses, an Israelite who had miraculously been saved from Pharaoh's decree that all male Israelite children be killed and who was actually raised in Pharaoh's very own household. Moses organized the Israelites, brought God's miraculous plagues upon the Egyptians, and, after a dramatic night in which the Egyptian firstborn sons were killed by divine intervention, led their long march to the land of Canaan. Trapped at a body of water called the Red Sea (not the same body of water as the one known by that name today), the Israelites were again rescued by God; the waters parted for them to cross, then closed again over the heads of the pursuing Egyptians. Later, the Israelites assembled at Mount Sinai, where God revealed Himself to them and charged them with a covenant according to which they were to be His chosen people and they were to obey His commands.

The fleeing Israelites did not take the more direct coastal route, where Egyptian forces were stationed, but went through the desert known today as the Negev. They first tried to enter the land from Kadesh-Barnea but were eventually forced to make an approach via the Transjordan region, where several small states—Ammon, Moab, and Edom—had recently been established by groups ethnically related to the Israelites. According to the biblical account, it was in the land of Moab that Moses died, though not before having transferred the leadership of the people to Joshua.

The Bible gives several different accounts of the conquest of Canaan by the Israelites. In some places, it says that Canaan was quickly conquered and divided among the twelve tribes—the descendants of the twelve sons of Jacob—in adherence to a plan prepared in advance. Other parts of the Bible suggest that the conquest was a long, unplanned process in which each tribe conquered its own territory. This latter version is better corroborated by archaeological evidence. Despite the discrepancies within the biblical account, archaeological remains do show widespread destruction of Canaanite towns in the

ABOVE: *The Crossing of the Red Sea*,
by Luigi Bernardino (1475–c.1532).

RIGHT: *Moses with the Tablets of the Law*,
by Guido Reni (1575–1642).

BELOW: A sulphur spring on the coast of the Red Sea,
opposite Suez. According to tradition, this is where the
Egyptians drowned while pursuing the Israelites.

MOSES

According to the biblical account, Moses, the son of Israelite slaves in Egypt, was abandoned in the Nile by his mother in order to save his life when Pharaoh decreed death for all Jewish newborns. He was discovered in his tiny box by Pharaoh's daughter, who adopted him and raised him in the palace. (The name she gave him is now known to be an Egyptian name, though the Bible explains it as meaning "drawn out of the water.")

As a young man, Moses killed an Egyptian because of his outrage at the mistreatment of Hebrew slaves by their Egyptian taskmasters, and had to flee to Midian. In the desert he encountered a bush that was in flames but miraculously unburnt; out of the bush, God spoke to him, ordering him to lead the Hebrews out of Egypt. When Pharaoh refused to permit the Hebrews to leave, God sent ten plagues to weaken them; after the last of these plagues—the killing of the Egyptian firstborn sons—Pharaoh relented. But three days later, Pharaoh and his troops pursued the fleeing slaves, cornering them at a body of water often called the "Red Sea," but correctly known as the "Sea of Reeds." When Moses stretched his magic staff over the waters, they parted, allowing the Israelites to cross; they then flowed together again, drowning the pursuing Egyptians. Moses led the people to Mount Sinai, and ascended the mountain to receive God's commandments.

Moses' intention was to lead the Israelites to the land of Canaan, which God had promised to give to them. But when the scouts he had sent out to explore the land returned with the discouraging report that the land was too fortified to be conquered, the people refused to go farther. For their lack of trust in Him, God then ordered the people to wander in the desert for forty years.

At the end of this time, after many adventures, Moses assembled the people near the east bank of the river Jordan and delivered a lengthy address to prepare them for taking over the land of Canaan after his death. He recapitulated the rules of conduct that they had taken upon themselves in service to God and warned them that if they proved unfaithful to these rules, God would exile them from the land. After naming Joshua his successor as leader of the Israelites, Moses ascended Mount Nebo and died, within sight of the Promised Land.

Moses, by Lorenzo Monaco (c. 1370–c. 1425).

Joshua Stopping the Sun, by Raphael (1483–1520). The painting depicts one of the most famous miracles in the Bible. During the wars against the Canaanites, God, at the petition of the Israelite leader Joshua, prevented the sun from setting so that the Israelites could complete the pursuit of their enemies.

thirteenth century B.C. and the creation of new, less elaborate settlements.

The Israelites settled the land in three regions (north, central, and south) that were separated by Canaanite enclaves, and in a fourth region (east) that was separated from the others by the Jordan River. Eventually, each tribe became established in a particular district. The main tribes were Reuben and Gad in the east; Dan in the north; Menasseh (whose territory also stretched eastward across the Jordan), Benjamin, and Ephraim in the central region; and Judah in the south. But Judah did not succeed in holding on to the town that was later to be called Jerusalem. Instead, this town was soon reconquered

by another migrant group called the Jebusites, who gave it their name, Jebus.

With the settlement in Canaan, the Israelites gave up the nomadic life of shepherds and instead established small towns where they turned to agriculture. The settlers cut forests, developed new techniques for making cisterns, and slowly began to work with tools made of iron, a material that was new to them. At this point, the tribes probably did not have a strong sense that they belonged to a single nation. The later Jewish tradition came to view the revelation at Mount Sinai as the moment when the Israelite nationhood was forged; but it is more probable that this concept of nationhood was a slow development that was only completed with the establishment of the monarchy at the end of the eleventh century B.C. However, even during the period of the conquest and settlement, there must have been links of importance between the tribes, for they were of similar descent and religious tradition. Some sort of formal, though loose, supratribal organization may even have existed—a compact that some scholars have called the Amphictyony; according to the Bible, the mobile sanctuary called the Ark of the Covenant would have been the central institution of this organization.

There is evidence in the biblical account that during the period between the settlement and the establishment of the monarchy—the twelfth and eleventh centuries B.C.—a tendency toward temporary coalitions between tribes and experiments with various kinds of leadership existed. In the Bible, this period is covered by an entire book, Judges, which tells colorful stories of individual tribal leaders who either exercised leadership over a particular tribe or region for an extended period of time or who achieved miraculous military victories. Particularly interesting are the stories of the war of Deborah and Barak against the Canaanites in the north; the adventures of Samson in his battles with the Philistines on the coast; the battles of Gideon against the Midianites, who had invaded the central region from Transjordan; and the battles of Jephtha against the Ammonites. The stories of Gideon and his son Abimelech may even represent a transitional stage from rule by tribal leaders to a type of monarchy.

But it was the pressure of the Philistines—who were settled on the southern coast—against the central tribes of Benjamin and Ephraim that led to the actual establishment of the monarchy. Because the Israelite tribes were too loosely organized to defeat the Philistines, they asked Samuel, a widely respected seer, to appoint a king to replace the traditional leadership (which usually consisted of a group of

Gaza, one of the five cities of the Philistines, and the scene of the adventures of Samson, as it might have appeared in biblical times.

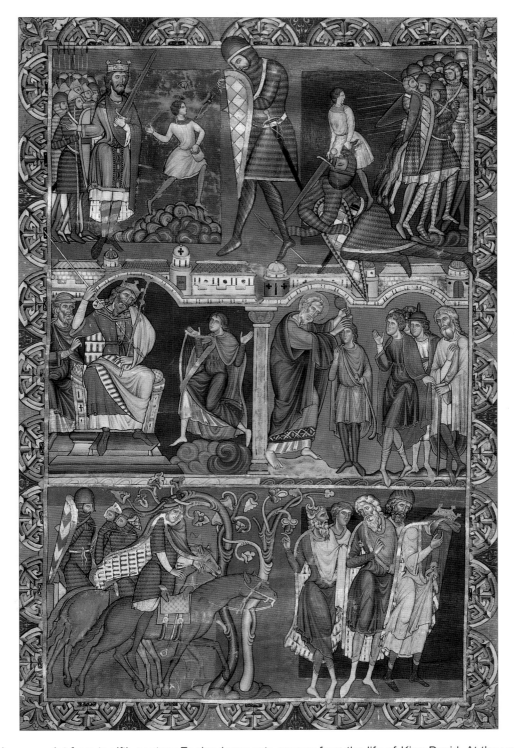

This illuminated manuscript from twelfth-century England presents scenes from the life of King David. At the upper right, David battles Goliath; on the left side of the middle panel, David plays the lyre for King Saul; the bottom panel depicts the death of Absalom, caught in a tree, and David mourning him.

elders or, occasionally, a single charismatic leader). The idea of a permanent, hereditary monarchy made the tribes feel more secure. Samuel chose a Benjaminite, Saul, who drove the Philistines out of the mountain territories but did not succeed in ousting them from Israelite territory altogether. He established a standing army and levied taxes, though he also continued to rely to a great extent on traditional tribal institutions and practices. But it appears that his rule must have been unsatisfactory to Samuel for some unknown reason, for he ended up losing the seer's support.

David, who as a young soldier had defeated the Philistine hero Goliath in single combat, became one of Saul's officers. His youth and popularity aroused Saul's jealousy, and when Saul flung a spear at him, he fled to nearby Philistea. There he gathered a militia that he used to help to protect the border settlements. After a period of service under a Philistine ruler, David established relations with the leaders of the tribe of Judah. Following Saul's death, which came about during a disastrous battle against the Philistines, Saul's son Eshbaal reigned over a reduced territory and David was anointed as king over the tribe of Judah. David soon acquired control over the other tribes as well and conquered Jebus, taking it away from the Jebusites. The city reverted to its earlier name, Jerusalem, and became David's personal estate as well as the capital of his kingdom.

With the accession of David (c. 1004 B.C.), the history of the Israelite monarchy truly begins. David eliminated the Philistines as a major power, though he never succeeded in completely eradicating them. By getting rid of the remaining Canaanite enclaves, taking control of Ammon and Moab in the Transjordan region, and defeating the Aramaean kingdoms in the north, David created a small but powerful empire that may have reached as far north as the Euphrates River. With access to both the Mediterranean and the Red Seas, with control over the two main highways for international commerce (the Sea Route along the coast and the Royal Route through the Transjordan), with good relations with the Phoenician kingdoms of Hamath and Tyre, and with the two world power centers of Egypt and Mesopotamia in a period of weakness, David's kingdom became an important force in the region.

David largely succeeded in his attempt to unify the tribes, despite continual opposition from separatist forces. Within his own tribe, there was sufficient opposition to his rule that even his son Absalom tried to overthrow him. David was forced to abandon Jerusalem and go to war against his own son, but Absalom, in his flight, was caught in a tree by his long, lovely hair, and in this helpless position he was ruthlessly killed—against orders—by one of David's men. David's lament for his rebellious son is one of the most poignant moments of his story. In David's declining years, his son Adonijah tried to oppose his determination to bequeath the kingdom to a younger son, Solomon. But David stood firm and ensured his decision by having Solomon crowned during his lifetime.

The kingdom came to a full flowering in the time of Solomon (c. 965–928 B.C.), whose reign was marked by prosperity, relative peace, and the expansion of the solid foundation established by David. Thanks to control of the trade routes, access to the two seas, and advantageous treaties with the Phoenician kingdoms of Tyre and Sidon, the Israelite kingdom became a major commercial power. The royal merchant marine sailed great

King David, by Marc Chagall.

DAVID

David was a boy from Bethlehem who was selected and anointed as king by the prophet Samuel, and who founded the dynasty of Judean kings. Samuel's intention was to replace King Saul with a more satisfactory leader. But David did not become king immediately. He came to Saul's attention by challenging Goliath, a huge Philistine warrior, to single combat and beating him with a sling. Saul took him into his army, then into his household as a musician, for David played the harp and sang beautifully, soothing Saul when his dark moods came upon him. But Saul quickly became jealous of David for his great popularity among the people. One night, when David was playing for him, Saul cast his javelin at him. David fled to the land of the Philistines and offered his services to the king of Gath, who gave him a fortress. Organizing a militia, David pretended to be raiding Judea, but he was actually fighting the Canaanites and biding his time. When Saul and his son Jonathan were killed in a battle with the Philistines, David returned to Judea and became king, first in Hebron over the Judeans, and shortly thereafter, in Jerusalem over all the Israelites.

David was a colorful, gallant, and not always virtuous leader. He demonstrated his gallantry by not killing his enemy Saul when he came upon him sleeping and helpless in a cave, as well as by caring for Saul's grandson Mephiboshet after the death of Saul and Jonathan. He had many adventures with women. Infatuated with Bathsheba, he had her husband sent to the front to be killed, so that he could marry her; for this, he was castigated by the prophet Nathan. He fought successfully against the Philistines, finally putting an end to the long-standing threat they had posed to the Israelites; he also conducted successful wars against Edom, Ammon, and the Arameans.

David made his capital at Jerusalem, which would be regarded by the Jews right down to the present as the geographical focus of their identity. According to one biblical account, he wanted to build a temple there but was prevented by a prophet, on the grounds that as a man of war, he did not have the right to do so.

A major upheaval of David's reign was the rebellion of his son Absalom, who had himself proclaimed king in Hebron. The threat was sufficiently great that David removed his court from Jerusalem and fled to Gilead, in the Transjordan. Absalom's troops pursued him there. But as he rode through a forest, Absalom was caught by his luxuriant hair in the low branches of an oak tree, and while he hung there suspended, one of David's men killed him, despite David's express instructions that he not be harmed. David's response to the notification that Absalom was dead is one of the most moving passages of the Bible.

Another child of David's had already died, the one first born to him and Bathsheba after David had brought about her husband's death. David and Bathsheba had another son, who was called Solomon. To guarantee that Solomon would succeed him as king, David had him anointed in his own lifetime.

According to ancient traditions, David, besides being a king and a warrior, was also a poet, the author of religious hymns. That is why many of the psalms, and sometimes the whole Book of Psalms, are attributed to him.

David Dancing Before the Arc, by Francesco Salvati.

Solomon's ships arrive in Phoenicia, whose merchants provided rare goods for his court in Jerusalem: gold, silver, ivory, apes, and peacocks (I Kings 10:22).

distances, exporting copper from the mines established by Solomon in the extreme south of the country and importing precious metals and other luxury items. The cultivation of trade with Arabia is evident in the biblical story of the visit of the queen of Sheba to Solomon's court. Horses and chariots were imported for resale to other local kings as well as for use in the new chariot corps that Solomon introduced. He even had special cities built for these corps to use as their bases.

The income from these trade activities was used to support a large-scale building program focused on the royal city, especially on the palaces and the Temple. For these projects, foreign architects and builders were hired and high-quality materials were imported. Solomon's foreign treaties, his marriages to the daughters of the rulers with whom he made these treaties (ancient Israel, like many Near Eastern

cultures, sanctioned polygamy), and his extensive imports of luxury items all contributed to a newly cosmopolitan Israelite culture, one that was far removed from the primitive conditions of earlier centuries. This period probably also saw the beginnings of a Hebrew literary culture.

But there were signs of trouble. Whereas David had relied on compulsory foreign labor, Solomon introduced a much-loathed system of compulsory labor service for Israelites. The building projects created a trade deficit with the Phoenician king of Tyre, which could only be made up by ceding certain towns to him. Furthermore, the tax burden began to impoverish the Israelite population. Certain tribes felt discriminated against and resented Solomon's favoritism toward the tribe of Judah. And priests attached to distant religious centers resented the expansion of the Jerusalem Temple and the diminution of their own status and prosperity. These sources of resentment led to several attempted rebellions toward the end of Solomon's reign.

After his death, Solomon's son Rehoboam was recognized by his own tribe, Judah, as the successor to the throne, but he failed to gain the allegiance of the northern tribes. Hence, the kingdom split: Rehoboam retained rule over the southern tribes of Judah, Benjamin, and Simon, but the northern tribes recognized Jereboam I, who had previously tried unsuccessfully to lead a rebellion against Solomon, as their leader.

For about two centuries, the people were divided into two kingdoms: the southern kingdom, called Judah, continued to be ruled by scions of the house of David; meanwhile, the relatively unstable northern kingdom, confusingly called Israel, was ruled by various individuals, some of whom were able to establish family dynasties lasting a few generations,

others of whom reigned only briefly before being assassinated. It must be noted that when discussing the period of the divided kingdoms, the term "Israelites" denotes only the inhabitants of the northern kingdom, while the term "Judeans" (from which the later term "Jewish" would be derived), denotes the inhabitants of the southern kingdom.

Jereboam I set about making a complete break with Davidic institutions. He established his capital at Shechem and restored two ancient sites of worship, at Beth El and Dan, to replace the Temple in Jerusalem, appointing new priests to replace those who might retain loyalty to the house of David. Contrary to the biblical account, Jereboam I did not introduce idolatry; rather, this accusation stemmed from southern opposition to his rule, and it was included in the biblical account under the influence of prophets loyal to the Davidic dynasty. Because of the southern kingdom's bitter opposition to Jereboam's secession, the two kingdoms were frequently at war.

Both kingdoms also had to contend with trouble from Egypt at various times, but for approximately the first seventy years after the division, their main external problems were with the other small states of the immediate vicinity. These states included the little kingdoms of Edom, Moab, and Ammon in the Transjordan; the Aramaeans in Damascus in the north; and the Phoenicians in Tyre and Sidon. All these states were constantly aligning and realigning themselves as one attempted either to gain the upper hand over another or to extract itself from the power of another. In the following discussion, we examine the reigns that are of special interest.

The northern king Omri established a new and successful dynasty in 882 B.C. Moving his capital to Samaria, he entered into treaties with Etbaal, the

ABOVE: A reconstruction of Solomon's Temple by John W. Kelchner, based on details given in the Book of Kings.

LEFT: The Prophet Isaiah, by Marc Chagall. The prophet is depicted at the moment of his consecration, when an angel purified his mouth by touching it with a hot coal.

THE BOOKS OF THE JEWS

In Hebrew, the Bible is called *Miqra*, or Reading. Sometimes it is called *Kitve Haqodesh*, or Scripture. But the most common name is *Tanakh*, an acronym standing for Torah (the books that are often called the Five Books of Moses), Prophets, and Writings, also sometimes called *Hagiographa* (meaning "sacred writings"). This name reflects the traditional division of the books of the Bible in the Jewish tradition.

The Torah consists of five books. It probably reached its final form during the Babylonian exile (586–538 B.C.), having been compiled over time from writings and traditions going back to 1000 B.C. or even earlier. According to tradition, it was given to Moses at Mount Sinai along with the Ten Commandments, which are included in it. The five books narrate the history of the descendants of Abraham, from the time that Abraham left Mesopotamia through the death of Moses. Genesis begins with the creation of the world and the flood. It then tells the story of Abraham, his sons Isaac and Ishmael (ancestors of the Jews and Arabs, respectively), Isaac's sons Jacob and Esau, and Jacob's sons, the ancestors of the tribes of Israel. Exodus tells how the Israelites were enslaved in Egypt, how they were miraculously rescued by Moses, and how they received the Ten Commandments and made a covenant with God at Mount Sinai. Numbers tells of their adventures in the desert during the forty years of wandering. Deuteronomy contains Moses' final addresses to the people before his death in the land of Moab. Exodus, Leviticus, Numbers, and Deuteronomy also contain the laws, both civil and ritual, of the Israelites. Leviticus consists almost entirely of ritual laws, and Deuteronomy contains an extensive recapitulation of both civil and ritual law.

The Prophets contains nineteen books. The first four (Joshua, Judges, Samuel, and Kings) contain an almost continuous narrative of the history of the Israelites from the time they entered the Land of Israel under the leadership of Joshua until they were expelled from it by the Babylonian king in 586 B.C. The next three books contain all of the speeches of the great prophets of Israel from the seventh and six centuries B.C.—Isaiah, Jeremiah, and Ezekiel—who admonished the kings and the people for their disobedience to God, and who also delivered God's promise of redemption after the disaster of the exile (the prophecies of consolation in Isaiah were actually by a different prophet, whose name is not known). These three books are followed by twelve small books by other prophets who lived during the same period but whose works were not as extensively or as accurately preserved.

The Writings is a miscellaneous group of books of varied nature. Psalms is a collection of 150 prayers in verse, many of which may have been recited by Levites as part of the temple service. Proverbs is a collections of maxims on religious and moral conduct. Job is a moral tale and a vast poem on the problem of why people suffer. Five small books known as the "scrolls" contain a love poem, a poem on the destruction of Jerusalem, a meditation on the meaning of life, a story of a Moabite woman who joined with the Jewish people and ended up becoming the ancestor of King David, and the story of how Queen Esther saved the Jews from the plots of a Persian courtier. Then follow the visions of Daniel, dealing with the exile and redemption, and the historical books of Ezra and Nehemiah. Both books deal with the period known as the Restoration; Nehemiah includes the personal memoirs of one of the governors of Judea in the period. The Hebrew Bible concludes with Chronicles, which recapitulates the history of the kings of Judea.

king of Phoenician Sidon. The alliance was sealed with the marriage of Omri's son Ahab to Etbaal's daughter Jezebel, introducing to the history of Israel one of the most interesting women to appear in the Bible.

Ahab continued Omri's policy of improved relations with Judah. The kingdoms went to war together against Aram-Damascus, but they quickly began to realize that an event on the world stage—the rise of Assyria—was far more threatening than any local rivalries. At the battle of Karkar in 853 B.C., the allies held off the Assyrian king, but the situation provided the opportunity for the people of Moab to free themselves from Israelite domination, an event recorded in the famous Mesha inscription, which may be seen today at the Louvre in Paris. The Aramaeans and Israel then fought again at Ramot-Gilead, a battle that brought about the death of Ahab, but apparently not an Aramaean victory.

During Ahab's reign, Israel had become an important force in the region; Judah also prospered, thanks to the temporary peace between the sister states. But Ahab—no doubt influenced by his strong-willed wife, who persecuted the prophets—had also permitted the expansion of Phoenician culture, including pagan practices of worship, into the northern kingdom. On account of these transgressions, Ahab and Jezebel were vehemently denounced by the prophet Elijah, who was supported by much of the populace. Ahab's son took over control of the northern kingdom after Ahab's death; but he in turn was later killed by a general named Jehu, who purged the northern kingdom of foreign cults and exterminated the royal family, killing the dangerous Jezebel.

During this time, Judah had also been troubled by a Phoenician woman, the redoubtable Athalia, wife of King Jehoram. The daughter of Ahab and Jezebel, Athalia attempted to introduce the Phoenician style of life and practices of worship into Judah, just as her mother had done in Israel. When Prince Ahaziah took over the throne after most of the royal family of Judah had been captured, Athalia subjected him to her control. She eventually seized power completely and had killed what was left of the royal family. Although Phoenician influence had been removed from the northern kingdom, she remained its advocate in the south; this aroused a great deal of resentment and led to a revolt in which she was killed.

Israel gradually dwindled to the area immediately surrounding Samaria. But then the Assyrians temporarily turned their attention away from the region, affording Israel's king at the time, Jereboam II, new opportunities for expansion. The southern kingdom also entered into prosperity during this period under King Uzziah, who conquered Edom (including the Bay of Eilat) and other neighboring territories.

The Mesha stele, from the end of the ninth century B.C. Named after the Moabite king who ordered its erection, the stele describes the battles of Moab and Israel. It is written in the Moabite language, which is very similar to Hebrew.

However, Assyria again became a great and threatening presence in the region. After the death of Jeroboam II, the northern kingdom degenerated into dynastic chaos and was forced to pay tribute to Assyria, as were the Judean kings of this time. Attempts to compel the Judeans to join an anti-Assyrian coalition failed. During 733–732 B.C., the Assyrians besieged and captured Damascus, took territories in the Transjordan and the Galilee, and later established a puppet king in Israel.

The end came for Israel when the entire region rose in revolt. The Assyrians retaliated with a campaign that included a three-year siege of Samaria. When Samaria finally fell in 722 B.C., the history of the northern kingdom was brought to a close. The inhabitants were exiled and, following a curious Assyrian practice, replaced by settlers from other territories that the Assyrians had conquered. This exile is known as the exile of the ten northern tribes.

Throughout these events, Judah was, on the whole, quietly submissive to Assyria. But when the situation had stabilized, Hezekiah, king of Judah, became part of an anti-Assyrian front. In addition to a series of reforms intended to rally national spirit around the house of David and the Temple, Hezekiah fortified Jerusalem, built the famous Siloam tunnel (which can still be visited today) to bring water within the walls in case of siege, and reorganized the army. The Assyrian king Senna-cherib soon descended on the Palestinian coast, destroying several Judean cities and exiling part of the population. He laid siege to Jerusalem, but soon thereafter abandoned it for reasons that have not been explained; the Bible attributes his departure to a miracle.

When Josiah came to the throne of Judah, in 640, Assyria was about to succumb to the Babylonians. He is famous for his religious reforms, which included repairing the Temple, wiping out idolatrous shrines from his territories, and generally rallying the people around the house of David. According to the biblical account, when the Temple renovations were in progress, a priest discovered an ancient scroll of the Torah (the five basic books of the Jewish religion, considered to be divinely revealed) containing instructions to center the cult exclusively on a single shrine, presumably in Jerusalem. This scroll is now believed to have been a form of the Book of Deuteronomy. Its promulgation led to the celebration of the renewal of the covenant between God and the people and to the elaborate celebration of the festival of Passover in Jerusalem.

Josiah sought to play a part in the fateful events taking place on the world stage by helping the Babylonians against the failing Assyrians. Egypt had sent an army to reinforce the Assyrians, and Josiah intercepted them with his troops at Megiddo. He was killed in the ensuing battle, and his death is what

LEFT: Two ivory lions from Samaria, the capital of the Northern Kingdom.

RIGHT: King Josiah promulgates the law, reading it from a book newly discovered in the Temple, while the false priests burn on an outdoor pyre.

brought Judah to the period of its final decline, for the next Judean king, Jehoiakim, would pay tribute to Egypt.

Judah was now caught between the two great powers of Egypt and Babylonia. Although the prophet Jeremiah repeatedly bade the last Judean kings to submit to Babylonia, Jehoiakim participated in an anti-Babylonian rebellion. Promised Egyptian aid never arrived. Nebuchadnezzar then besieged Jerusalem, and Jehoiakim died during the siege. His son Jehoiachin was exiled to Babylonia in 597 B.C., along with his court and other high officials. In Babylonia, Jehoiachin was soon released from captivity. He was treated with respect and allowed to retain his royal title. The treatment he enjoyed there would come to have great significance at a much later stage in Jewish history.

Meanwhile, Nebuchadnezzar set up Josiah's son Zedekiah as puppet king of Judah, but despite admonition from Jeremiah, Zedekiah rebelled and joined a regional revolt supported by Egypt. Some help did come from Egypt this time, but the Babylonians brought the city under siege once again, this time to the point of destruction, which occurred in 586 B.C. The Temple was burnt to the ground. Zedekiah's sons were killed before his eyes, after which he was blinded and brought in chains to Babylonia. Much of the population was exiled, and the territories were invaded by neighboring states. A small area of Judean settlement was permitted to remain around Mizpeh under the governorship of Gedaliah ben Ahikam, but he was murdered by former Judean officials. With his death came the end of Judean sovereignty and the end of the first part of the history of the Jews. The memory of the Davidic state would become one of the defining historical themes of Jewish identity; the hope for its eventual restoration would become the foundation of the idea of the Messiah.

TOP: The city of Babylon, as reconstructed by Uckhard Unger.

ABOVE: The Babylonian conquerors destroying the Temple's bronze basin, as depicted by James J. Tissot (1836–1902).

CHAPTER TWO

THE SECOND JEWISH STATE

*J*eremiah had predicted that the exile from Judah would be brief, and in 538 B.C. the events that would make his words come true occurred. The Babylonian empire, which had so recently replaced the Assyrian empire as the dominant force in western Asia, was itself replaced by the rising new empire of the Medes and Persians under the dynamic leadership of Cyrus. Cyrus reversed many policies of the Babylonians: he gave the exiled Judean king Jehoiachin a permanent government pension; he proclaimed that a group of Judean exiles could return to Jerusalem to reestablish a state there under his protection (this proclamation forms the concluding verses of the Hebrew Bible); and he announced his intention to rebuild the Temple, empowering Zerubbabel, a descendant of Jehoiachin, to begin the work. These events launched the period known as the Restoration.

The empire established by Cyrus lasted until 330 B.C. Our only sources for Jewish history in this period are the biblical books of Ezra and Nehemiah, and scholars disagree considerably on the interpretation and chronology of the events recorded in them. The age is therefore often called the "dark period" of Jewish history. It is known that the benevolent policy of the Persians toward the revived Judean state continued. But our sources do not give us a clear impression of the tiny new kingdom of Judah, which consisted of not much more than Jerusalem itself.

A prime concern of the returning Judeans was to reestablish the central institution of their national identity—the Temple. Work was begun but was soon halted because of the interference of the population of the territory of the former northern kingdom (Israel). An altar was constructed and the daily sacrifices resumed. But some time passed before construction of the Temple and of the city walls could begin again.

OPPOSITE: An elderly Jew reading the Yom Kippur prayers in a St. Petersburg synagogue. The large print on the upper part of the page is the text of the prayer in Hebrew; the denser print on the lower half of the page is a translation into Yiddish.

ABOVE: Cyrus the Great (r. 559–530 B.C.), founder of the Persian Empire, king of the Medes and Persians, and restorer of Jerusalem.

Not all the exiles chose to return. The deposed king Jehoiachin, for example, remained in Babylonia, as did many of the Judeans who, by this time, had firm roots in the land of their exile. Jeremiah, who had fled the destruction of Jerusalem to go to Egypt, had advised the exiles to pray for Babylonia, telling them that their welfare depended on its welfare. This attitude was to serve as religious legitimation for those who chose to cast their lot with the Babylonian empire and its successors, the Medes and the Persians. The Judeans who chose not to return to Jerusalem became the nucleus of the oldest and longest-lasting Jewish Diaspora community, that of Iraq, which existed until 1951. ("Diaspora" refers to the Jewish communities scattered throughout the world.) It was these people in Iraq who first developed the idea that it was possible to retain one's identity as a Judean without actually living in Judah, and this concept is the practical basis of what we call "Jewish identity" to this day.

We should not forget that not all the dispersed Judeans were located in Babylonia. Many had fled to Egypt and had established a community there. And they were not the first Jews to reach Egypt. From ancient papyrus documents, we know that some Jews actually arrived in Egypt before the destruction of Jerusalem and that there was a Jewish military garrison at Elephantine, an island in the Upper Nile. This garrison remained in existence at least until the conquest of Egypt by Alexander and perhaps considerably longer.

How could one retain Judean identity in a foreign country, speaking a different language and living in a manner that was indistinguishable from the majority population? Suddenly, it became urgent to establish a code of Judean practices before they could be forgotten, and to instill these practices in the children of the exiles. Here, modern observers differ in their interpretation of events, but all agree that something very significant occurred. Traditional believers maintain that the Judean leadership in exile in Babylonia, headed by Ezra the Scribe, restored and promulgated the Torah—where it was in danger of being forgotten—

and saw to it that the exiles would continue to observe its precepts. Historians maintain that the Judean leadership compiled surviving records of the historical and religious traditions of Judah and made them the foundation of Judean identity. In other words, they actually composed the Torah at this time as a compilation of earlier documents from the time of the monarchy. According to either interpretation, this was an event of permanent significance for the Jews, for it established Jewish identity on the basis not of statehood or language but rather on the basis of religious practice.

The Torah was promulgated in the new Judean state as well. At an unknown date in the fifth century B.C., the Persian ruler authorized Ezra the Scribe to go to Judah and to declare the Torah there as the law by which the Judeans would govern themselves, for the Torah contains not only ritual laws, but a civil code as well. The Aramaic document authorizing the establishment of the Torah as the law of the land has been preserved in the Book of Ezra, and it remains thrilling reading to this day; its legal language created an institution that would last for more than two thousand years. But even more exciting is the account in the Book of Nehemiah of how the Torah was promulgated in the city of Jerusalem.

On the first day of the seventh month of the lunar-based calendar (this date would become the New Year for later Judaism), a great assembly was held in the main square of Jerusalem. A special wooden platform had been constructed for the purpose, and the leaders of the community stood in a row on either side. As Ezra the Scribe unrolled the book (books were made in scroll form in those days), the assembled people all rose. He pronounced a blessing and proceeded to read from the early morning until noon, as the people listened to the first public reading of the Torah. Afterward, they promised to observe its laws, and the day was brought to a close with feasting, celebration, and the exchange of gifts.

Nehemiah, who was the governor of Judah for two periods of time during the fifth century B.C., is mentioned as having been present at the ceremony, but again, there is no agreement as to exact chronology. As a young Judean exile, Nehemiah had been a courtier of a Persian king. When reports of the miserable condition of Jerusalem reached the court, he was deeply affected by the fact that the city walls had not been rebuilt. He begged to be sent there as governor with a mandate to restore the city, and the king agreed. Late in his career, Nehemiah wrote his memoirs; this book, which eventually became part of the Bible, is a precious human document of this obscure period.

In Jerusalem, Nehemiah encountered opposition from the governors of neighboring districts, who naturally feared that the fortification of Jerusalem would give it the power to dominate the region. These governors tried to stop him through mockery, political maneuverings, and even attempts at assassination. Despite this resistance, the walls of Jerusalem were completed in 445 B.C.

Existing sources tell us practically nothing of the entire century following the fortification of Jerusalem.

This is the last long period that cannot be accounted for. The little information that is known about this time is that Judah was ruled by a governor who was appointed by the Persians and by the high priest.

In 334 B.C., the young Macedonian ruler Alexander began his march of conquest, which would sweep away with startling rapidity all the kingdoms—great and small—of the Middle East, from Egypt to the Indus River. This event was of vast importance to Jewish history, for all the Jewish communities that were in existence at the time came under Greek control, and the Jews were introduced to a culture that would stimulate, entice, threaten, challenge, and enrich them until our own time. Alexander passed through Palestine in 332 B.C., and though he did not visit Jerusalem, he did apparently meet with the high priest and confirm the rights that the Judeans had under the Persians.

Alexander the Great died soon after conquering India, and his empire was divided among his generals. Babylonia, the home of the largest Diaspora community, fell to Seleucus (who was based in Syria)

A megillah, a scroll containing the Hebrew text of the Book of Esther used in the synagogue on the festival of Purim. The festival commemorates the collapse of a plot to kill all the Jews of the Persian empire.

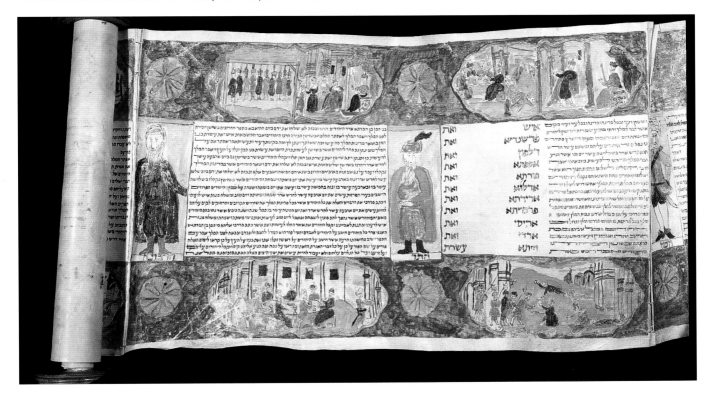

THE BOOKS OF THE JEWS

BEN SIRA

The Wisdom of Ben Sira, also known as Ecclesiasticus, is a collection of maxims and advice for conducting a life of wisdom and moderation. It includes a historical survey of the great leaders of Israel, from the patriarchs through the kings and early leaders of the Second Commonwealth, down to Simon the Righteous, who was high priest—and therefore head of the Judean state—around 200 B.C. Simon is vividly described as he emerges in splendor from the Holy of Holies, the secret inner room of the Temple, which was entered only once a year for the ceremonies of Yom Kippur. The Wisdom of Ben Sira was written in Hebrew in Simon's lifetime. Because the Jews did not consider it sacred, the Hebrew original was lost; fortunately, it was translated into Greek in Egypt and eventually became part of the Apocrypha, books that the Catholic Church considers to have true teaching even though they are not part of the Bible itself. In this way, it was preserved among Christians. The Hebrew original was one of the remarkable finds preserved in the Cairo Geniza (see chapter four).

THE BOOKS OF THE MACCABEES

Four books preserved in Greek narrate events related to the Antiochene persecutions. These books, like the Wisdom of Ben Sira, were not considered by the Jews to be part of the Bible, but they were collected by early Christians into a group of books that came to be called Apocrypha.

I Maccabees and II Maccabees tell the story of the uprising against the Hellenistic kingdom of Syria at the time of Antiochus IV, including the exploits of the five sons of Mattathias. Despite the similarity of their names, they are separate accounts of the history of

Judea in the period; II Maccabees was abridged from a much longer work. III Maccabees is not a historical work but rather a miracle story. It tells of the persecution of the Jews of Alexandria by one of the Ptolemid kings of Egypt of the period, who decreed that the Jews were to be trampled to death by elephants in a hippodrome. The Jews were saved by warrior-angels who appeared in the hippodrome, terrifying the king, his court, and the elephants. IV Maccabees tells of the persecution of the Jews under Antiochus IV. It is especially famous for the story of the seven brothers who refused the king's bidding to eat ritually forbidden food, and who were all killed; the story came to be known as "Hannah and Her Seven Sons," and was widely known among both Jews and Christians. The book gives so much gruesome detail of the torture and suffering of the martyrs that its name gave rise to the English word "macabre."

The angel leading the army of the Maccabees, in a woodcut by Gustave Doré.

and his heirs, while Egypt fell to Ptolemy and his heirs. Since Palestine lay between these two powers, it was a bone of contention between them, and this meant wars and hardship for the inhabitants. For most of the third century B.C., the Ptolemids were in control of Palestine, but there was constant war with Syria, and by 200 B.C. the Seleucid ruler of Syria, Antiochus III ("the Great") had gained control. This was a fateful event for the Judeans.

During the second century B.C., Greek states of the Near East had to face the expansion of the Roman republic in the eastern Mediterranean. The Seleucids needed large amounts of money and raised it however they could, even by attempting to plunder the treasures of the Judean Temple (because temples were considered inviolate, it was common for many ancient peoples to store national treasures in them). Antiochus IV (r. 175–164 B.C.) actually did succeed in looting the Temple, with the help of the high priest himself.

This bizarre event came about because there was contention among the Judeans themselves. The arrival of the Greeks under Alexander had not only signified a change of political control but had also introduced a new and prestigious culture to the Middle East: Hellenism. The Greek language, Greek fashions, and especially Greek thought swept Egypt, Palestine, and Iraq, forging a common culture that was adopted by many of the subject people, especially by the upper classes throughout the region. The Jews of Egypt, who by this point formed a significant community, were largely Hellenized, and it was not long before they translated the Torah into Greek. Many of the Judeans became Hellenized during the century of Ptolemaic rule, and since it was primarily the upper classes that were attracted to the cosmopolitan ways, the hereditary priesthood was among them.

A Judean named Jason set in motion a disastrous series of events when he bribed Antiochus IV to depose the high priest and make him high priest instead, promising to raise more money in taxes and to turn Jerusalem into a Greek city. Much to the consternation of the traditionalists, Jason had a gymnasium built there in which people—in keeping with the Greek fashion—exercised naked. This institution became the focus of social life. Jason did not last long as high priest: contenders for his position soon outdid one another in their attempts to bribe Antiochus IV, and it was one of these contenders who led Antiochus to the treasures. By this time, Jerusalem had become completely Hellenized, with Antiochus taking the final step by outlawing such traditional religious practices as circumcision and the observance of the Sabbath; he also forced Judeans to eat pork, which was contrary to their religious beliefs, and in 167 B.C., he rededicated the Temple as a shrine to Olympian Zeus. The situation was complicated by Antiochus's mad pretensions to divinity. He took as his royal title the epithet "Epiphanes" ("the manifest god"), which the Jews soon mockingly distorted to "Epimanes" ("the madman"). Antiochus IV has gone down in Jewish history as the first ruler who systematically persecuted the Jews; from his reign date the first stories of Jewish martyrdom.

This event was something completely new in the history of the Jews. When the Babylonians had destroyed the Temple in 586 B.C., it was a political event in which a large state swallowed up a smaller one, destroying its capital and burning the shrine that was the rallying point of its ruling dynasty. Although the actions of Antiochus IV also had a political aspect, they were primarily intended to alter the culture of the Jews, outlawing their ancestral religion and forcibly turning them toward Greek practices. It was the first instance of religious persecution in Jewish history, and many Jews responded with martyrdom. But many actually supported Antiochus's policies and, motivated by their own social aspirations, helped put them into effect.

A revolt was not long in coming. An obscure family of priests headed by a man named Mattathias led guerrilla warfare. After Mattathias's death, the work was carried on by his five sons, known as the Maccabees. Judah the Maccabee liberated Jerusalem in 164 B.C., and the festival of Hanukkah was instituted to commemorate the event. But the wars of the Maccabees were far from finished. The family continued to fight against the Syrians, with one brother after another being killed. Finally, in 142 B.C., the Syrians were forced to recognize the Judeans as an independent nation with Simeon, the last of the "glorious brothers," as the high priest and ruler. In 140 B.C., a great assembly convened in Jerusalem, confirming Simeon in his powers and establishing a hereditary dynasty that would come to be known as the Hasmonean dynasty. For the first time in more than four centuries, the Jews had an independent state and an independent ruler; it was a glorious moment, but one that was destined to last less than eighty years.

The increasing weakness of the Seleucids afforded the early Hasmonean high priests opportunities to expand their territories. The ones who accomplished the most were John Hyrcanus (r. 134–104 B.C.) and Alexander Janneus (r. 103–76 B.C.), who brought much of the territory belonging to the biblical southern and northern kingdoms, including important parts of the Transjordan, under Judean control. But the Hasmonean high priests became increasingly Hellenized as their power grew. Both of those just mentioned, for example, had Greek names, and another, Aristobulus I (r. 104–103 B.C.), adopted the title of king. Many people resented these developments, and parties soon formed. Some, like the Essenes, rejected the Hasmonean dynasty completely. They were otherworldly sectarians who lived a semimonastic existence near the Dead Sea and in small communities throughout the country. It is widely believed that the Dead Sea Scrolls (discovered in 1947 and still the subject of much controversy) reflect the religious beliefs of the Essenes and derive from the Essenes' library of religious books.

The Pharisees, on the other hand, who represented the national religious traditions, wavered in their support depending on the policies of the particular rulers; more often than not, however, they were in opposition to the high priests. Serious conflicts between the ruling dynasty and the Pharisees arose in the reigns of both John Hyrcanus and Alexander

TOP: A Judean eight-wick oil lamp dating from the fourth or fifth century A.D.

ABOVE: Among the Dead Sea Scrolls are copies of most of the books of the Bible. This is a page from the Book of Isaiah.

THE TEMPLE OF JERUSALEM

The hill known as the Temple Mount was traditionally regarded as the spot where Abraham built an altar on which to sacrifice his son Isaac at God's command. Upon conquering Jerusalem from the Jebusites, David built a shrine there, and in the next generation his son Solomon built the splendid temple that was the main ritual center of the Judean kingdom until its destruction in 586 B.C. The dedication of the new Temple, about sixty-five years later, was an occasion for mixed emotions: amid the shouts of joy from the young people present could be heard the weeping of the very old, who could still remember clearly the beauty and the glory of the original Temple and the pain of its destruction.

After various attempts at renovation, a major project for enhancing the Temple was instituted by Herod in 19 B.C. The work went on for forty-six years, and when it was done, people said, "Anyone who has not seen the Temple of Herod has never seen a beautiful building." This is the building that was destroyed in A.D. 70 by the Romans. Its site has been occupied since the seventh century A.D. by the beautiful Mosque of Omar; its sparkling golden dome is one of the most beautiful and distinctive features of the Jerusalem skyline.

The maintenance of the Temple and its rituals was a very important part of the life and economy of the people of Judea throughout the period of the Second Temple. Individuals offered personal sacrifices in connection with their personal prayers and out of gratitude to God for events in their lives, such as the birth of a child or recovery from illness. On three annual festivals, especially Passover, thousands of pilgrims brought lambs, goats, and doves for festival sacrifices; these were presented at the Temple for ritual slaughter and then eaten as part of the festival meal.

Several taxes were levied to maintain the building, the sacrifices, and the Temple personnel. The most characteristic of these was the half-shekel contributed annually by every Judean. This particular tax was paid loyally, even by those Judeans who were no longer living in Judea.

The main ritual of the Temple was the offering of sacrifices. Every day, two lambs were slaughtered and burned on the great altar, one in the morning and one in the afternoon. The people believed that these offerings were demanded by God and that performing them guaranteed their national welfare. The daily sacrifice was accompanied by the kindling of the famous seven-branched candelabrum, the burning of incense, the pouring of wine, and the blowing of the horn. The main rituals were performed by the hereditary priesthood; there was also a corps of singers whose hymns accompanied the sacrifice. Some of their hymns may still be read in the Book of Psalms. At the conclusion of the sacrifice, the priest would bless the people with the words preserved in the Book of Numbers:

> May the Lord bless you and keep you.
> May the Lord shine upon you and grant you favor.
> May the Lord raise His countenance to you and grant you peace.

Some of these rituals are still performed in the synagogue. The blessing of the priest is included in the daily service, and the blowing of the horn is still performed on the Jewish New Year (Rosh Hashanah). But since the Jewish tradition permitted the offering of sacrifices only in the Temple of Jerusalem, this practice was discontinued soon after the final destruction of the Temple in A.D. 70.

Janneus. But under Alexander's successor, Queen Salome Alexandra (r. 76–67 B.C.), the Pharisees were actually in control of the government and were able to institute their policies and traditions, which would eventually develop into rabbinic Judaism.

Salome's death was followed by dynastic chaos, which was resolved only by the Romans, who invaded under the leadership of Pompey in 63 B.C. Although the newcomers did not at first do away with Hasmonean rule, they did reduce its territories and limit its powers. But international developments led the Romans to put an end to the dynasty in 37 B.C. by appointing Herod, a former governor of Galilee, as king of Judea.

The Temple Mount in Jerusalem. The wall on the right is the Wailing Wall, a portion of the retaining wall of the Temple Mount that has survived since Herod's construction. Known in Hebrew as the Western Wall, it is the central object of veneration for religious Jews, a large group of whom may be seen gathered at its foot to worship. Looming above it, on the site of the Temple, is the Dome of the Rock, one of the great holy places of Islam.

Herod was descended from a non-Judean family; his father had held a governorship under Janneus and Salome. He came to power through his relationship with powerful Roman leaders; his appointment as king of Judea was ratified by the Roman Senate on the recommendation of Mark Antony and Octavian (later Augustus). Completely loyal to Roman interests, Herod was a sagacious ruler who had cultivated powerful friends in Rome, including the emperor Augustus himself. These attributes permitted him a long and successful reign. The Romans expanded the territories under his control, so that again the Jews dominated most of the territory of old Israelite kingdoms. Herod reorganized many of the institutions of the Hasmonean state, curtailing the power of both the Sanhedrin (the highest deliberative body) and the high priesthood. But since he was not of priestly descent, Herod had to appoint others to the latter office. Determined to maintain control, he was careful to appoint only men loyal to himself and to limit their terms of office.

Herod was a truly cosmopolitan ruler, whose reign was similar in style to that of other Hellenistic kings in the eastern territories of the Roman Empire. He amassed wealth and cultivated luxuries of every kind, and he engaged in extensive and impressive building projects, including the harbor at Caesarea, fortresses at Herodium and Masada, and many projects in Jerusalem, which he turned into a magnificent capital. He rebuilt the Temple on an unprecedented scale, to the pride even of Jews who disapproved of his decadent way of life. (A fragment of its retaining wall remains standing today and is known as the Wailing—or Western—Wall.) Moreover, Herod was a cultivated man and his court was full of non-Jewish visitors from abroad, including Greek scholars and writers. Altogether, he was one of the most powerful, multifaceted, and interesting figures in Jewish history. To this day, he is known as Herod the Great.

His successors were not able to maintain his kingdom, though, and in A.D. 6 the Romans reorganized Judea as a Roman province and appointed governors, most of whom were foreigners. The best-known of these was Pontius Pilate, who governed from A.D. 26 to 36. His involvement in the execution of Jesus—one of the central events in the history of Western religion, and one that has plagued the Jews until this very day—was of no importance whatsoever to the immediate political life of Judea. At most, it may have increased slightly the tensions between the Roman administration and the population, which stemmed primarily from heavy taxes, inflexible Roman rule, and the presence of hostile Roman soldiers in the country.

Unrest continued to mount under the rule of the unstable Roman emperor Caligula, who ascended to the throne in A.D. 37, and who, like Antiochus IV, believed himself to be a deity and demanded divine honors from his subjects. Attempts to set up a golden image of him in Jerusalem led to massive opposition by the populace, but the plan died with the death of the emperor in A.D. 41.

The western gate of Sebaste, built by Herod the Great.

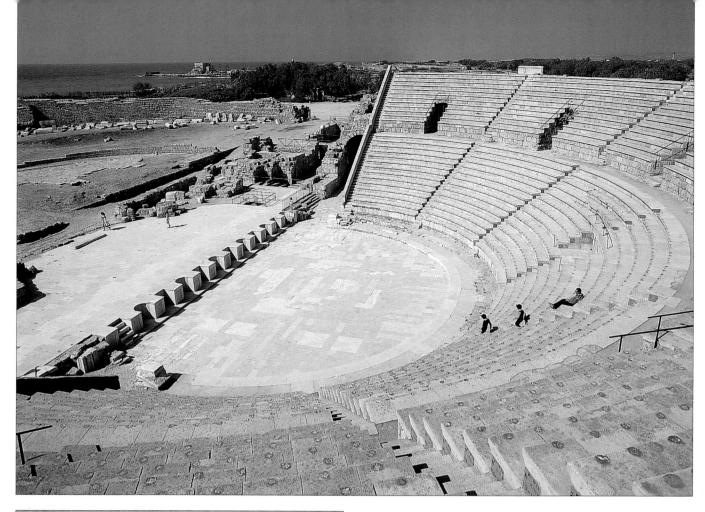

Judea had only one brief moment of independence during this whole dismal period leading up to the great war with Rome. The emperor Claudius, who reigned from Caligula's death until A.D. 54, appointed Agrippa, a grandson of Herod, as king of Judea, so that for three years (41–44) Judea ceased to be a mere province. Agrippa had a close personal relationship with Claudius, which gave him some flexibility in managing the affairs of the state, and he was closer in sympathy to traditional Jewish ways than his grandfather had been. Accordingly, Agrippa was extremely popular with the Pharisees and unpopular with the non-Jews of Palestine.

ABOVE: Roman amphitheater in Caesarea, built between 22 and 10 B.C.

LEFT: Masada, Herod's fortress on a hill overlooking the Dead Sea, and the last Judean outpost captured by the Romans after the Judean War.

Upon his death, a new series of procurators was appointed, and the discontent of the population mounted. There were clashes between Jews and Greeks in Caesarea, and extremist messianic groups multiplied. Severe measures by the procurators failed to establish order, and the Roman administration of Judea broke down completely in the days of Florus, the last procurator, who served from 64 to 66. By this time, Rome was bitterly hated by the Jews because of its continued heavy hand, its idolatrous emperor cult, its supervision of the activities of the Temple, and its favoritism toward the non-Jewish population. In A.D. 66, a revolt broke out. The priests stopped offering the sacrifice for the welfare of Rome, and the people destroyed the Roman garrison in Jerusalem and defeated another Roman army outside Jerusalem.

Nero, who was emperor at that time, sent an army under Vespasian to crush the revolt in the Galilee and Transjordan. But Vespasian could not pursue his initial success immediately because of the death of the emperor Nero in 68. In 69, Vespasian became emperor, and in 70 the war was resumed under his son Titus, who quickly took Jerusalem and burned Herod's magnificent temple to the ground. Other fortresses fell soon thereafter. Among them was Masada (near the Dead Sea), which was manned by members of an extremist Judean party called the Zealots. Unwilling to yield at any cost, the defenders committed suicide just before the Romans made their final assault. Thus ended the last vestiges of the second Jewish state. There would not be another until our own time.

Though Judea was a small state, the Romans saw the suppression of its revolt as an important and glorious victory. Celebrating with great pomp, they paraded the Judean captives and sacred ritual objects from the Temple through the streets of Rome. The event was even commemorated with a victory arch, which still stands in what is left of the Roman forum. On this arch is a carved depiction of the procession, including the seven-branched candelabrum of the Temple. But like the Temple itself, the great forum of Rome is now a ruin.

Just as the ancient Judeans had weathered the destruction of their kingdom and Temple, the Jews who experienced this second destruction endured. In fact, the latter were actually in a better position to retain their Judean identity, for by this time Judaism had achieved a gradual shift from a mere political identification to a religion. A religion defined by beliefs, writings, and rituals is quite portable, and the Jews had already carried their identity and religion to most parts of the Roman world.

One of the main centers was Egypt, especially Alexandria, where the Jews formed an autonomous community headed by an official called the ethnarch and later by a council of elders. Under the Ptolemid successors of Alexander, they had generally lived peacefully, but under Roman rule tensions mounted, climaxing in anti-Jewish riots in A.D. 38. The riots

A Roman gold coin minted in A.D. 71 in honor of the victory over Judea. The emperor Vespasian is depicted on the obverse; the seated woman on the reverse represents Judea in bonds; the inscription is *Iudaea Capta*—"Captive Judea."

were partly due to the negative attitude of the Roman governor, Flaccus. The Jews of Alexandria generally were Greek-speaking and, though loyal to Jewish traditions, were quite Hellenized. This mixture of cultures produced a lasting literary monument in the work of Philo of Alexandria (c. 20 B.C.–A.D. 50), who tried to reinterpret the Bible and Jewish religious practices in the light of Greek philosophy. Alexandrian Jews were well informed about Greek literature as well, and some of them wrote Greek poetry and plays.

The Jews of Alexandria revolted against the Roman government on the death of the emperor Caligula (41); in sympathy with the Judean revolt against Rome in 66, and during the empire-wide rebellion of Jews from 115 to 117. On this last occasion, the great synagogue was destroyed and the community went into decline.

The Arch of Titus, erected in the Roman forum in commemoration of the victory over Judea. The frieze depicts the triumphal procession of Judean captives and trophies seized from the Temple by the victors, prominent among which is the seven-branched candelabrum.

Judaism was also well rooted in Babylonia by this point. The Seleucid rulers had been replaced in 129 B.C. by the Parthians, who allowed the descendants of the Judean exiles a fair degree of autonomy. After the Romans, who were a constant threat to the Parthians, took control of Palestine, the Jews were seen as natural supporters of the Parthian regime, so relations between them and the government were generally benign. Under these conditions, the Jewish community grew in numbers and wealth. Even in this early time, many Jews made the transition from agriculture to trade.

The Jews of Babylonia were permitted to administer their own affairs; the office of the exilarch, the head of the Jewish community, may already have been in existence at this early time. According to tradition, this position was always occupied by a descendant of the ancient Judean royal house of David (the members of this distinguished family had been in Babylonia since the exile of Jehoiachin, the penultimate king of Judah). These exilarchs were considered high government officials and were treated with great dignity, just as Jehoiachin had been treated during the time of Cyrus. The institution of the exilarchate was extraordinarily long-lived, surviving through Sasanid and Islamic rule and finally petering out in the eleventh century A.D.

By A.D. 70, the Jews had spread far beyond the Middle East. We have seen that as early as 586 B.C., they had formed important communities in Babylonia and Egypt. Gradually, they settled farther and farther from their place of origin. We find important Jewish communities in Asia Minor, in the city of Rome, and in the Roman provinces, including Spain. Although the main center of Jewish identity would remain Palestine for centuries to come, the means to be a Jew were now available across the world. But Jews in the Roman Empire were still defined politically as Judeans. They continued to send their half-shekel tax annually for the maintenance of the Temple, and when the Jews of Palestine revolted, anti-Judean riots took place in many parts of the empire.

CHAPTER THREE

THE JEWS IN ROMAN PALESTINE AND SASANID BABYLONIA

The destruction of the Temple necessitated changes in religious doctrine and practice, for the Temple had been the center of the chief official form of Jewish worship. But the way had already been partially cleared for these changes. For about a hundred years before the destruction of the Temple, a class of lay experts in religious law had been acquiring more and more influence. Although the hereditary priesthood retained great prestige, these specialists, called rabbis, played an ever greater role in directing religious life.

Legend accounts for the transfer of religious life from the Temple and its priesthood to the rabbis and their teachings in this way: when Jerusalem was under siege by the Romans, one of the great rabbis, Johanan ben Zakkai, had himself smuggled out of the city in a coffin and brought before Vespasian, who, amazed at his audacity and impressed with his wisdom, granted him the right to establish an academy in Jabne, a small Judean border town. For the forward-looking rabbi, this meant that the physical city, the Temple, and even political sovereignty could be dispensed with as long as there was a way of ensuring the transmission of religious traditions. The study of the Torah, as well as the oral traditions that had accumulated around it, would become the central religious duty and the focus of religious education in the future development of Judaism. Thus, the foundation was laid for the preoccupation of Jewish culture with intellectual activity.

Ben Zakkai taught that even the Temple service could be replaced, for already the ancient prophets had said that God prefers the service of the heart to the sacrifice of animals. Some kind of prayer services had probably existed before the destruction of the

A scroll of the Torah, the first five books of the Bible, in its elegant case. Such scrolls are always handwritten in Hebrew on parchment or vellum with a quill or a reed. They are used for the formal reading of scripture in the synagogue service. This one is from Morocco.

Temple, but now these prayers were regulated and declared a duty for each person. Synagogues, which had played a secondary role in Jewish religious practice while the Temple was standing, now became the focus of public worship and religious instruction, besides serving as places of assembly. Thus, although the generation that experienced the destruction was thoroughly traumatized, the basis for continuity was laid fairly early.

And the destruction of the Temple did not mean an end to Jewish life in Palestine. Many Jews were killed and taken captive, and many fled; but for the most part it was only the upper classes and the priesthood who were affected. There was no mass expulsion at this time. The Jews were punished by the imposition of a tax—known as the *fiscus Judaieus*—consisting of two drachmas annually paid to the Roman treasury instead of the smaller half-shekel tax that the Jews had always paid to their own Temple. Imposed on Judeans throughout the Roman Empire, this tax was the cause of great resentment. As time passed, though, it came to be tolerable to most Judeans.

But Roman rule was harsh, and revolts by Jews continued to break out in different parts of the empire. In A.D. 117, the Jews of Cyrene, an important Roman port in what is now Libya, rose in revolt. Soon the Jews of Alexandria engaged in a revolt as well, to which the Romans responded by destroying their famous, huge synagogue (it was so huge that teams of callers were employed to serve as human amplifiers in order to relay the readings and sermons to the congregation). Even in Palestine, there was a revolt under the governor Quietus.

The climax of this series of revolts—the uprising of Bar Kochba—had truly severe consequences for the Jews. The emperor Hadrian, a great lover of antiquities and of architecture whose reign extended from 117 to 138, conceived a plan to rebuild Jerusalem as a Roman city. Its name was to be Aelia Capitolina, and it was to be dedicated to Jupiter. This plan was intolerable to the Jews, and the revolt that ensued was supported by prominent rabbis, includ-

A coin from the Bar Kochba revolt. The Hebrew inscription says that the coin was minted in A.D. 133–34.

ing the revered Rabbi Akiva, who apparently traveled abroad to raise funds for it. Bar Kochba (of whose origins, and of how he came to lead the revolt, nothing is known) proclaimed the independence of Judea and issued coins engraved with such inscriptions as "Year Two of the Freedom of Israel"; he acted in every way as the ruler of the Jews and head of the troops. The revolt lasted three years, from 132 to 135, ending with a Judean defeat. The remnants of Bar Kochba's troops were besieged in Bethar and massacred there.

If the Judeans thought that they had been punished in the year 70 with the burning of their Temple, now, sixty-five years later, they felt the full might of Roman revenge. The Jewish population of Judea was decimated, and a new population of non-Jews was imported to replace them. So many Jewish captives were taken and sold as slaves that they depressed the prices in the Roman slave market. Jews were prohibited from even entering Jerusalem, now called Aelia Capitolina. Moreover, Hadrian outlawed many Jewish practices altogether, especially the public teaching of the Torah (although this order was strictly imposed only in the Galilee) and circumcision. He

THE BOOKS OF THE RABBIS

Most of the important books of rabbinic Judaism were written during the period covered by this chapter, including the first survey of rabbinic law, the Mishnah, written by Rabbi Judah the Patriarch around A.D. 200. Divided into six parts and composed of short paragraphs designed for easy memorization, the Mishnah deals with laws of agriculture, festivals, marriage, civil law, Temple ritual, and ritual purity. The Mishnah also contains a treatise of general religious advice, dealing with the importance of the study of both the Torah and the rabbinic tradition as well as with moral conduct and good manners. This treatise is known today as "The Chapters of the Fathers," and contains Hillel's famous maxim: "If I am not for myself, who am I? And if I am only for myself, what am I? And if not now, when?"

The Mishnah states the law on each subject concisely and often cites divergent opinions, but it rarely states the reason for a ruling. Tracing the biblical or logical basis for a ruling, distinguishing similar cases, defining the exact applicability of mishnaic rulings—all these were the topics of discussion among the ancient rabbis and their disciples. In the fifth century, these discussions were compiled into books called the Talmud. One such compilation, known as the Palestinian Talmud, was made in Tiberias; another, made in Iraq, is known as the Babylonian Talmud.

Other books of the period covered by this chapter contain abridged versions of sermons preached by the rabbis based on biblical texts. Such homilies, called *midrashim* (the singular is *midrash*), were collected in books like Genesis Rabba, which contains midrashim on the Book of Genesis. Such books are important sources for understanding the religious thought of the rabbis, and are still scoured by rabbis seeking sermonic material. Individual midrashim are also scattered throughout the Talmud. Midrashim often contain fanciful versions of biblical stories, fables, and folktales. The most famous midrash collection by far is the one contained in the Haggadah, the booklet read aloud in traditional Jewish homes each year at the Passover seder. The first part of this book is a collection of ancient homilies on verses from the Bible dealing with the enslavement of the Jews in Egypt and how they were saved.

A table set for the Passover seder, a family ritual commemorating the exodus from Egypt and the ancient annual Passover sacrifice. The book is a Haggadah, the traditional reading for the ceremonial dinner. The plate contains foods that are consumed in connection with the ritual or are placed there in commemoration of ancient rites.

even changed the name of the province from Judea to Syria-Palestina.

There are a number of stories ascribed to this period by the rabbinic tradition about rabbis who were martyred for observing the laws or for teaching the Torah. The most famous of these stories relates the martyrdom of Akiva, whose flesh was raked from his body with iron combs. Many scholars and others fled, swelling the Diaspora communities. Judeans flooded Rome, where we can still see their underground burial places in the catacombs; they swelled the small existing Jewish settlements in Gaul and Spain; and they even traveled as far as the Rhineland. Nearer to Judea, the Jewish communities of Asia Minor also waxed populous.

The severe measures of Hadrian did not stay in full force for long, however. Later in the century, a compromise was reached between Rome and the Jews. The practice of the Jewish religion was again permitted, and the government even sanctioned the naming of a central rabbinical authority, a person called the patriarch, and a central court, called the Sanhedrin. Both of these institutions had existed in different forms during the Temple period. The official positions were now held exclusively by rabbis, who exercised broad administrative and judicial functions with Roman authorization. The patriarch, endowed with a substantial amount of power, could appoint both rabbis (who often functioned as judges) and teachers and could collect a tax not only in Palestine but throughout the Roman Diaspora. Looked upon as the central Jewish religious authority, the patriarch also fixed the religious calendar each year for all these communities. With Judea depopulated of Jews and Jerusalem still closed to them, the center of Jewish life moved north to the city of Tiberias in the Galilee.

The basis of this compromise was an unspoken agreement that the Jews could practice their religion and have limited autonomy as long as they controlled their extremists and prevented outbreaks of violence. In exchange for their tranquillity, the Jews were also exempted from military service and excused from appearing in court on the Sabbath.

With this encouragement, the rabbis were able to put their stamp permanently on Jewish life and religion. Toward the end of the second century, Rabbi Judah the Patriarch produced a collection of laws covering every aspect of the rabbinic tradition: laws regulating agriculture, festivals, marriage, civil law and procedure, laws governing worship, and laws of ritual purity. This book, known as the Mishnah, became the fundamental textbook for rabbinic Judaism. Nearly all vestiges of other approaches to Judaism that had existed during the period of the Jewish state disappeared because of the wide influence of the patriarch and the official status of rabbinic Judaism. The Mishnah was a key step in establishing rabbinic Judaism as the dominant force in Judaism until modern times. Later rabbis have continued to study the Mishnah and to organize their lectures around its precepts.

Roman rule over Judea continued to be fairly mild once the Jews had, for practical purposes, abandoned hopes of sovereignty. More and more, they were treated like the other peoples of the empire; in 212, the Jews (together with most other inhabitants of the empire) were granted Roman citizenship. The fortunes of Judea followed more or less those of the empire at large, for good and for ill, throughout the third century, and the Jews shared the economic decline that would later be seen as an early herald of the empire's collapse in the fifth century.

Meanwhile, in Babylonia—which still had the most important Jewish community outside Palestine—the new Persian empire, under the Sasanid dynasty, took control in 226. The Jews there continued to prosper, except for a period of trouble under the reign of Shapur I (r. 241–72), which stemmed partly from a conflict with the Zoroastrian priests, who acquired much influence under this dynasty. But the fundamentally favorable situation continued in force: Rome was the great enemy of the Sasanids, and the Jews could be counted on to support the Sasanids against the Roman Empire, which had destroyed Judean sovereignty, devastated its capital, and desecrated its sacred objects. Although the Babylonian Jews had not suffered personally, and probably no longer thought of

LEFT: The synagogue at Capernaum, on the north shore of the Sea of Galilee.

RIGHT: Floor mosaics from the ancient synagogue of Hamat, near Tiberias.

themselves as Judeans in exile, they remained linked to their Palestinian brethren.

One of these links was the dependence of Babylonian Jewry on the religious authorities of Palestine. The Torah and the oral traditions of its interpretation were studied in Babylonia, but the Palestinian schools dominated; for example, as mentioned earlier, the patriarch annually determined the calendar of the festivals for the entire Diaspora. Although some Palestinian scholars—disciples of Akiva—fled to Babylonia during the Hadrianic persecutions, there-

by raising the status of the Babylonian schools, the authority of the patriarch in religious matters was dominant and extended even to the territories controlled by the exilarch.

Early in the third century, two men established Babylonia as a major center for the cultivation of religious traditions and law. These were Samuel, a wealthy local scholar who enjoyed a good relationship with Shapur I, and Rav, a Palestinian rabbi who emigrated to Babylonia in 219. It was Rav, who had been a student of Rabbi Judah the Patriarch, who

introduced the Babylonian Jews to the study of the Mishnah. Soon there were two academies—one at Sura, the other at Pumbeditha. These schools would remain in existence as rivals until the eleventh century.

The Babylonian schools benefited from the weakness of the Roman Empire in the third century, because deteriorating economic conditions drove Palestinians eastward. This motion reduced the population subject to the patriarch and increased the population subject to the exilarch, as well as enhancing the power of the two Babylonian academies. As a result, the Babylonian schools became more and more independent.

In fact, by the end of the third century, Palestine, though still the world center of Jewish culture, was no longer the main center of Jewish population. The patriarch would remain the central religious authority for world Jewry almost until the collapse of the Roman Empire in the fifth century, but Jewish life thrived in the Persian empire—under the Sasanids in Babylonia—and in the great cities of the Roman Empire such as Alexandria, Antioch, and Rome.

The next fateful development for the Jews of Palestine and for the Roman Empire in general occurred when the emperor Constantine I (r. 306–37) adopted Christianity and made it the religion of the Roman Empire. We cannot recount here the complicated story of the rise of Christianity from Jesus' obscure circle of followers to the overwhelming force in world history that it became, but two points about this process are directly relevant to the history of the Jews.

One is the obvious fact that Christianity emerged out of Judaism, and that, in its early period, Christianity had to expend a great deal of energy defining itself as being something different from

ABOVE: Wall paintings at the synagogue of Dura Europos, in Syria, c. A.D. 239.

LEFT: Interior of the synagogue of Dura Europos.

Judaism. Christianity soon came to see itself not merely as the national religion of a small Roman province, with members scattered in a worldwide diaspora, but as a world religion whose mission was to unite all men in a single belief. In this, it differed fundamentally from Judaism. True, Judaism did proselytize, sometimes vigorously, until prohibited by the first Christian emperors from doing so; and Judaism did gain adherents among the Roman nobility, sometimes as full converts but more often as loosely affiliated "godfearers" (there are occasional

LEFT: Constantine I (c. 280–337), known as Constantine the Great, the Roman emperor who converted the Empire to Christianity and moved its capital to Byzantium, site of Constantinople (now Istanbul).

BELOW: Sarcophagus from Rome. Though completely Roman in every other stylistic detail, this relief has a seven-branched candelabrum, representing the famous candelabrum of the Temple, instead of the expected portrait of the deceased.

JOSEPHUS

Josephus's life bridged the periods before and after the destruction of the Second Temple. Born about A.D. 38 in Jerusalem, Josephus belonged to an aristocratic priestly family related to the Hasmonean kings. Well educated both in the traditions of the priesthood and in Greek language and culture, he was selected at the age of twenty-five to travel to Rome on a political mission. His mission was successful, and Josephus was profoundly impressed with Rome itself. When the Judean-Roman war began in 66, he was appointed commander of the Galilee. But there was local opposition to his appointment, and in any case the country was not prepared for war. The decisive battle for Josephus was the defense of Jotapata, which fell to the Romans. He fled with forty men to a cave; the men agreed to kill one another rather than fall into the hands of the Romans, but Josephus managed to escape and surrender to the Romans.

Josephus was treated leniently by the Roman commander, Vespasian. According to Josephus's own account, this was because, when brought before the commander, he foretold that the latter would soon become emperor. As we saw in chapter two, Vespasian was, in fact, recalled to Rome upon the death of the emperor Galba in 69, where he assumed the throne. When Vespasian was declared emperor in Caesarea, Josephus was released and went to Alexandria. When Titus replaced him as commander in Judea, Josephus accompanied him.

Josephus tried to play the role of negotiator between the Judean rebels and the Roman commander, but his position was untenable, since the Judeans regarded him as a traitor and the Romans as a spy. He finally settled in Rome, where he was granted Roman citizenship and a pension by the emperor. There he lived until sometime after A.D. 100, hated by the Jews of both Palestine and Rome.

But Josephus was not merely a traitor. Though assimilated into Roman society, he remained attached to his origins, and this inner loyalty is reflected in his writings. He was the author of four important books in Greek, two of them quite extensive, dealing with Judean affairs. The first is *The Jewish War*, written to promote the interests of Vespasian and Titus, his son and successor as emperor; the book tells the story of the Judeo-Roman war in great detail in an effort to display the virtues of the two general-emperors. His second book, *Jewish Antiquities*, was intended to defend the Jews against Roman contempt for them (see chapter two). Josephus's approach is to demonstrate that the Jews are an ancient people with long and distinguished traditions. *Against Apion*, his third book, is another refutation of the attacks of certain Roman anti-Semites, in which Josephus attempts to prove the moral superiority of Judaism over Hellenism. The fourth work is his autobiography, written to defend himself of charges by Romans that he was an enemy of Rome during the Judean war. All these books evince pride in his Judean origins and traditions, and, thanks to them, we have a precious store of information about ancient Judea that is not otherwise available.

Titus and Josephus, from an illustrated manuscript of Josephus's *The Jewish War*.

reports of first-century Roman ladies lighting Sabbath candles). But Judaism saw itself primarily as the religion of a particular nation with its home in Palestine. This strong national element, and Judaism's growing view of itself as a system of religious law with a heavy burden of ritual regulations did not give it wide appeal. Thus, Christianity, which was at first seen correctly by the Romans as a variety of Judaism, had to put distance between itself and the mother religion in order to attract more followers.

The second point involves the fact that as the Romans became more familiar with Jewish life and Jewish practices—through their occupation of Palestine and through the presence of Jews in Rome and other parts of the empire—a tradition developed of mocking and attacking exotic Jewish practices. Philosophers and intellectuals found Jewish religious practices irrational; the observance of the Sabbath came under especially forceful attack. Thus, by the fourth century, there was already in existence a sizable body of anti-Jewish literature in Latin and Greek, some of it by influential writers such as the historian Tacitus.

During the third century, the Roman emperors had persecuted the Christians, creating a spirit and ideology of martyrdom among them. The Romans came to be able to distinguish between Jews and Christians, exempting Jews on the whole from discriminatory regulations aimed at eliminating Christianity. When the situation reversed itself in the fourth century and Christianity came to power, the Christians unleashed their accumulated rage on the pagans and Jews alike. One element that was particular to the Jews, though, was the Christians' exploitation of the old anti-Jewish Roman sentiments, which they used to distance themselves violently from the mother religion and to punish Jews for not adopting the new religion. The fathers of the Christian Church actively preached hatred of Jews and Judaism. It is important to understand that modern anti-Semitism is deeply rooted in the early Christian centuries and that it has antecedents in Roman antiquity.

During the fourth century, the situation of the Jews in the Roman Empire deteriorated: marriages were prohibited between Jews and Christians; only Christians were allowed to own Christian slaves (effectively ruining Jewish landowners, for all large-scale agriculture in the Roman Empire was dependent on slave labor); Jews were prohibited from holding public office; and they were prohibited from building new synagogues. The patriarchate, already weakened, was extinguished in 429, ending the last vestige of the dominance of Palestine over Jewish life. The pattern was set for discriminatory regulations against Jews that would be standard throughout the Middle Ages and that to some extent would govern Jewish-Christian relations in Europe until the eighteenth century. These regulations were not always enforced, but they were considered correct.

Some of the Church leaders in this period and later wanted to outlaw Judaism completely and compel the Jews to accept conversion or death, just as the Romans had tried to outlaw Christianity in the third century. In Spain, the Gothic king Sisebut gave the Jews the choice to accept baptism or leave the kingdom. Fortunately, Saint Augustine (354–430) provided a rationale for permitting the continued existence of Judaism in the midst of a Christian world. He preached that for their obstinacy, the Jews should be abased, humbled, and crushed; but they should be granted the minimum conditions for existence, because their status as a dispersed and humiliated people would prove the truth and superioriy of the Christian religion. Furthermore, as bearers of what Christians were now calling the "old" testament, the Jews played the role of witness to the earlier divine revelation, which Christians believed predicted the coming of Jesus. To support his argument, Saint Augustine quoted the Psalms: "Do not destroy them, lest my people forget." Originally written as the Judean king's curse on his enemies, Augustine applied the verse to the Jews themselves. This grudging attitude, confirmed as official Church policy by Pope Gregory I (590–604), would be seen in later centuries as a generous one.

Jewish intellectual life did continue in Palestine. The fourth century saw an important literary development in the compilation of the Palestinian (sometimes incorrectly called "the Jerusalem") Talmud, a collection of academic debates and commentaries on the Mishnah. During this period, various rabbis also made collections of sermonic material, in abbreviated form, which is known as midrash. These works have all become classics of rabbinic scholarship and are studied to this day. From the fourth to the seventh century, there was an explosive development of Hebrew liturgical poetry, which was to become an important feature of Jewish literary creativity in the Middle Ages. In Babylonia during this time, the rabbis made their own compilation based on the Mishnah, known as the Babylonian Talmud. For reasons that will be discussed in chapter four, the Babylonian Talmud came to be thought of as "the" Talmud in the Middle Ages. It remains today the main textbook for the training of rabbis.

There were even a few bursts of political activity in Palestine during this period. The Jews of Palestine twice attempted to rebel, once in the fourth century and again early in the seventh, when relief from Christian oppression seemed to be in sight in the form of an invasion from the friendly Persian empire. But true and long-lasting relief would come from the unexpected rise of a new world power: Islam.

ABOVE: A group of seminarians studying the Talmud.

RIGHT: The first page of the Babylonian Talmud. The actual text of the Talmud is in the middle column, with its first word in a special frame. The other columns contain commentaries and notes by medieval and early modern rabbis.

CHAPTER FOUR

THE JEWS IN THE ISLAMIC WORLD, PART I (622–1500)

*F*or centuries, the great rivals in the Middle East had been Rome and Persia. The division of the Roman Empire into a western and an eastern empire (later to be known as the Byzantine Empire) was finalized in 364; as Rome had fought the Parthians in the east, so Byzantium had fought Sasanid Persia. By the beginning of the seventh century, the empires were exhausted from centuries of fighting, and in this moment of weakness a new force from Arabia entered the arena.

The Arabs were desert nomads and town-dwelling traders inhabiting the Arabian peninsula. Located on the margin of the two great empires, they sometimes served in these empires' armies and sometimes engaged with them in trade.

Muhammad (c. 570–632) was an Arab trader from Mecca who was deeply impressed by his encounters with monotheistic Jews and Christians. Experiencing visions and prophecies, he believed that he had been chosen to disseminate God's word—essentially the same monotheistic message as that given to Jews and Christians—among the Arabs. He established a small religious state in Medina, converting the townspeople there and many of the neighboring Arabs to his new religion, called Islam. After his death, the Arabs carried out raids in the adjacent regions, bringing their new religion with them. Such was their zeal, and such was the weakness of the Persian and Roman empires, that vast territories quickly fell into their hands. By

Mecca, the birthplace of Mohammad. In the foreground is the sanctuary with the Kaaba, the holiest shrine of Islam, in the center.

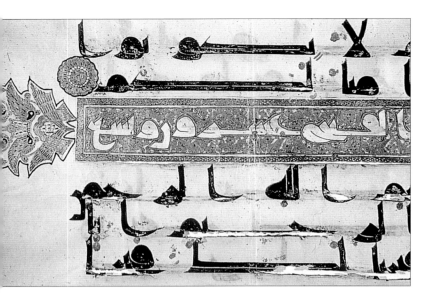

TOP: Page of the Quran in Kufic script.

ABOVE: Page of the Quran in Thuluth script.

the middle of the eighth century, they had toppled the Persian empire, wrested all of Egypt from the Byzantines and all of North Africa from the Goths, and had advanced through Spain to the Pyrenees.

This conquest was of supreme importance to the Jews, for it put many of the largest Jewish communities—including those of Babylon, Egypt, and

Spain—into a single political system for the first time in centuries. Furthermore, it brought instant relief from the grinding humiliation of life under hostile Christian rule. The Arabs did not embark on the conquest—as is commonly thought—with the intention of converting the world to Islam. There were cases of religious compulsion, but on the whole the conquered populations of the Middle East and Mediterranean world that converted to Islam did so simply because it was the easiest and most natural thing to do, just as it made sense to adopt the Arabic language. Although Islam, like Judaism and Christianity, was completely intolerant of paganism, Jews and Christians who preferred to retain their ancestral monotheistic religions were permitted to do so.

This is not to say that their lives were easy. Triumphant Islam insisted on regulating the religious lives of the subject Jews and Christians, and rules were instituted governing their status. Tolerated under the title of *dhimmis*, or "protected subjects," both peoples were required to pay special taxes in return for toleration. They were also subject to certain humiliating restrictions, which were partially derived from the Christian anti-Jewish regulations of the late Roman Empire. Dhimmis could not hold public office, own Muslim slaves, or build new synagogues or churches; furthermore, they had to wear distinguishing clothing, and dhimmi men could not marry Muslim women.

For the Christians, these rules served as a source of terrible humiliation and were probably a stimulus to conversion, which would free them from the degradation. For the Jews, though, the rules were actually a relief, for they showed that the Jews' right to inhabit Islamic territories and pursue their livelihoods was recognized by Islam and guaranteed by the rulers. This was a big improvement over their status under Christianity, where these rights were either only grudgingly recognized or not recognized at all and where the only theoretical basis of the Jews' right to exist was the humiliating logic of Saint Augustine. Besides, the rules were often ignored in actual practice. Furthermore, the Jews were not the

Mosaic depiction of a tree with wild animals from an Umayyad palace near Jericho.

only or even the most numerous group to suffer discrimination of this kind. As mentioned earlier, the Christians, who by far outnumbered Jews in the Muslim world, were restricted as well. In fact, the religious status of the Christians was more problematic for Muslims. Because of the doctrine of the Trinity, Muslims could never quite trust the Christian claim to be monotheistic; and Christian icons and crucifixes were deeply offensive to Islam, which abhorred images as potential objects of idolatry. Thus, on the whole, the Christians probably suffered more discrimination than the unambiguously monotheistic Jews.

Although the Byzantine empire prospered during this time, it was constantly on the defensive against Islamic armies. The western Roman Empire had collapsed in the face of the barbarian invasions of the fifth century, as a result of which western Europe was now sunk into the Dark Ages. The territories

conquered by the Arabs, though, were forged into a mighty world empire, unified by the Arabic language and the Islamic religion. We sometimes forget that the period we call the Dark Ages was only dark for a small part of the world. For the Islamic territories, the period from the seventh to the thirteenth century was a true golden age, and most of world Jewry was in a position to benefit from it.

The Muslims confirmed the favorable semiautonomous position that the Jews of Babylonia had long enjoyed under the Persians. The Babylonian Jews fared particularly well since the Muslims chose Iraq early on as the center of their empire and built their capital at Baghdad in 762. Thus, the most important Diaspora community found itself at the center of a world empire, and its leader, the exilarch, was a member of the court of the caliphs (as the Muslim rulers were called). This made the exilarch, at least in theory, not just the head of a local

Diaspora community, but the head of world Jewry, with power to raise taxes and appoint judges and teachers throughout the empire.

The early Muslims had little appreciation of agriculture, but they understood and encouraged trade. This attitude affected Iraqi Jews, who gradually shifted from agricultural villages to towns and became traders. Though quite different in its causes, this process complemented the one that had already occurred in the Byzantine Empire, where Jews had been shut out of large-scale agriculture. Thus, by the end of the eighth century, most Jews in the Muslim empire were engaged in trade and crafts, and their communities were gaining wealth and power.

The academies of Sura and Pumbeditha now attracted students from, and emanated religious teaching to, the rest of the world. Soon these centers of education moved to the capital at Baghdad. Their leaders were called *geonim* (singular, *gaon*, meaning "splendor"), which is actually an abbreviation for a more grandiose title that means "the President of the Academy of the Splendor of Jacob."

The geonim tried to unify religious practices for Jews worldwide through formal opinions on religious questions that they would issue (called *responsa*, and similar to Islamic *fatwas*). Because of an accident of history—namely, the fact that the Babylonian Jews were on the spot when the Muslims decided to make Iraq the center of their empire—the Babylonian Talmud, rather than the Palestinian Talmud, became the authoritative source for Jewish law for all time. The role of the geonim became so important that the whole period of Jewish history from the seventh to the eleventh century is known as the geonic period.

One of the geonim who wrought great changes in Jewish intellectual life was Saadia ben Joseph (882–942). Although the Jews, like all the conquered peoples, had adopted the Arabic language long before, Saadia was the first important rabbinical authority to use Arabic extensively in his books on religious matters. Thus, he is practically the founder of Judeo-Arabic literature, which was to have a long history. He also translated the Bible into

Arabic; wrote a detailed commentary on it; and wrote the first book of Jewish theology, *The Book of Beliefs and Opinion.*

During his lifetime, Saadia engaged in extensive literary battles with various Jewish sectarians. One sect that he attacked vehemently in his writings was that of the Karaites, founded by a scholar named Anan ben David who in the late eighth century had attempted to break with centuries of rabbinic tradition and to reestablish Judaism on the basis of the Bible alone. The Karaites, whose name means "People of the Scripture," believed that everyone should explore the Bible independently to determine religious law. This attitude was attractive to many Jews—especially those in the distant parts of Persia—who were dissatisfied with rabbinic leadership. It became an alternate variety of Judaism, and it has survived, though in very reduced numbers, until our own time. However, it did not remain as freewheeling as its original doctrines would imply. In practice, the Karaites, like the non-Karaite Jews, developed a uniform system of religious observance and codes of religious law, though the actual details were much different. Despite the rigidity of some of their practices, the Karaites had many adherents during the Middle Ages. Saadia and the other rabbis did everything in their power to brand Karaism as heresy and to eradicate it.

Saadia's career is important because he represented a new direction in Jewish intellectual life and a new type of rabbi. Being fully conversant in the Arabic language and thoroughly educated in Arabic literature, he had access to a wide range of intellectual activities that had never been available to earlier rabbis or that had not attracted their interest. Muslim scholars had absorbed literary ideas from such great ancient civilizations as India, Persia, and Greece, and had explored science and philosophy; they translated multitudes of works from the ancient languages into Arabic, meditated on them, and developed their ideas in new ways. All this contact with the thought of other peoples—especially Greek philosophy—instilled in many Muslim intellectuals a broadness of outlook that enabled them to discuss matters of religion on an even level with Jews and Christians, even though both of the latter were branded as non-believers by official Islamic doctrine. Like Saadia, other Jews were affected by this intellectual ferment, and the new intellectual life was soon reflected in Jewish books.

A tenth-century Jew with a knowledge of Arabic was in a position to explore vast treasures of world culture. Saadia began the process of synthesizing Jewish traditions with the results of centuries of scientific and philosophical studies. This daring intellectual adventure would become characteristic of the Jews in the Muslim world, putting them in the vanguard of Jewish intellectual life worldwide, just as the Muslims themselves were the vanguard of general intellectual life in this period.

Jewish life in Iraq continued on a fairly even keel, but declined in importance with the declining fortunes of the empire, which had weakened by the tenth century. The last gaon to enjoy worldwide authority was Hai, who died in 1038. Shortly after that, the Jewish community of Iraq lapsed into obscurity until modern times, as Iraq itself moved away from the center stage of Islam.

During the heyday of Islam, the Spanish Jewish community was spectacularly successful. The Jews of Spain were saved from the Christian king's edict outlawing the practice of Judaism by the Islamic invasion of the eighth century, and they recovered quickly under the benign Islamic rule. By the tenth century, some of them had accumulated considerable wealth through trade and the manufacture of textiles. During that century, the local ruler proclaimed himself formally independent of the empire centered in Baghdad, took the title "caliph," and expanded his capital in Cordoba into a magnificent city. One of his courtiers, a Jew named Hasdai Ibn Shaprut (Ibn is Arabic for "son of," equivalent to "ben" in Hebrew), gathered around himself a circle of Jewish intellectuals, including writers and poets, and encouraged the development of Hebrew poetry. Hasdai was the first of what are known as courtier-rabbis, men who hold public office in the overall community while at the same time serving as leaders of the Jewish community.

The Jews had a long tradition of poetry designed for use in the synagogue, but the idea of secular poetry in Hebrew was new to them. It was actually

ABOVE: The interior of the great mosque of Cordoba, one of the architectural marvels of the Muslim world.

RIGHT: One of the entrances to the great mosque of Cordoba.

View from above of the great mosque of Cordoba looking southward over the Guadalquivir and its Roman bridge. The massive structure jutting out of the mosque's roof is a Gothic cathedral built inside the mosque after the Christian conquest of southern Spain.

an imitation of the Arabic fashion. Poetry was popular among the Arabs to an extent hardly imaginable in our world, where poetry is completely marginal. In promoting Hebrew poetry, Hasdai added another element to Saadia's intellectual heritage of incorporating elements from world culture into Jewish life. In fact, poetry about love, wine drinking, gardens, and the joys of life came to be the most characteristic feature of Spanish Jewish culture under the rule of Islam; the poets adapted Arabic literary fashions in the writing of religious poems as well. Modern scholars of Hebrew literature think of this period as the Golden Age of Hebrew poetry.

One of the most interesting men of the period was Samuel the Nagid, who rose from obscurity to become the right-hand man of the prince of Granada in the eleventh century. (In this period, the main cities of Spain had become independent princedoms.) Samuel had been trained both as a rabbi and as an Arab intellectual. He could write poetry in Arabic and in Hebrew, and he was adept at managing the complex politics of the small courts of Muslim Spain. For a number of years, he was the de facto ruler of Granada and he may have had some military responsibility. Even though Granada was a tiny state, the fact that a Jew was in charge of it was a source of enormous pride to the Jews—and anger for the Muslim population. Samuel managed to bequeath his power to his son, Yehosef; but he could not bequeath his skills, and Yehosef was killed in a massive Muslim uprising against the Jews in 1066. A large-scale, murderous anti-Jewish riot was for the most part an anomaly in the Muslim world of this period. Clearly, Samuel and his son had crossed the line of tolerability in exercising power over Muslims.

The Jewish community of Muslim Spain did not merely peter out, as did that of Iraq. Instead, it was obliterated in the 1140s by an invasion of the

Almohads, a fanatical Muslim regime from what is now Morocco. For only the second time in the history of Islam, there was severe and systematic intolerance toward non-Muslims (the sole prior incident had occurred in early eleventh-century Egypt). The Almohads outlawed both Christianity and Judaism in their territories, and the Jews either assimilated or fled.

But Islam was actually in the process of being expelled from Spain. New Christian states had been formed in the north and were gradually driving the Muslims out. Toledo had already fallen to the king of Castile, and many Jews found refuge there. At first, the Jews were welcome in the newly Christianized territories—though this welcome would turn to rancor by the fourteenth century.

Among the Jewish families to flee Cordoba in the twelfth century was that of Maimonides, probably the most famous Jew of the Middle Ages. Maimonides was only a boy when his father, a famous judge, took his family on a series of journeys that would end in Egypt. As we have seen, Egypt

had always been a major Jewish center, and it became particularly important when a new dynasty took control of it in the tenth century and built the city of Cairo. The new ruler, like the ruler of Spain, took the title "caliph," and one of his chief advisers was a convert from Judaism. He and his successors generally treated the Jews favorably.

We are particularly well informed about the Jews of Egypt in the Middle Ages because of a peculiar circumstance. The Jews held it to be religiously improper to destroy any writing that might have the name of God in it or that had any religious significance. In practice, this rule was extended to include anything written in Hebrew letters, leading to a general disinclination to discard any written material at all. Thus, such items were either buried or simply stored when they were no longer needed. The Ben Ezra synagogue, located in the old city of Fustat (adjacent to—but now within—Cairo), had a storeroom used specifically for written matter (the *geniza*). When this storeroom was opened around

SAMUEL THE NAGID

Samuel the Nagid was one of the most versatile and famous Jews of the Middle Ages. Born in Cordova in 993, he first achieved prominence through his mastery of Arabic literary style, which won him positions first in the court of the governor of Malaga, and later in the court of the prince of Granada, which was an independent state. As a courtier, Samuel was deeply enmeshed in the turbulent and dangerous politics of the time; he often went to war with the troops of Granada against the neighboring states of Almeria or Seville, and he may even have served as a general. During long periods, he was left to manage the affairs of the state of Granada alone, because its prince, Badis, would neglect his duties entirely.

Samuel was also a Judaic scholar. He wrote books on religious law and Hebrew grammar, as well as biblical commentaries. And as if that were not enough, he found time to write Hebrew poetry as well. He is the first truly great poet of the Hebrew Golden Age. Many of his poems describe the battles in which he participated, and these tend to reflect a certain unease with this role. Yet his poetry is exuberant and strong, embracing life with all its possibilities and dangers. Because he was a man who combined political power, warfare, and poetry, he saw himself as a latter-day King David:

They ask "How can you praise the God
   on high?"
I say, "The David of the age am I."

A traditional portrait of the Jewish philosopher Maimonides.

1890, material of inestimable value was discovered. Containing books, letters, contracts, bills of sale and shipping, marriage contracts, poems, children's writing exercises, sketches, and incantations, the storeroom held a cross-section of the life of writing from the tenth century to the thirteenth. The material is so vast, so hard to decipher, and so fragmentary, that even a century later the study of it is far from complete. But what has been done permits a detailed look not only at intellectual life but also of commercial and everyday life—information that is not available for any other part of the Muslim world. The Ben Ezra synagogue has recently been renovated and may be visited in Cairo. The documents may be viewed at libraries in Oxford and Cambridge in England, in New York, and in a few other places.

When Maimonides arrived in Egypt, he was an outsider, but thanks to his great expertise in many fields, he became a celebrity whose opinion on religious law was sought from far away—much to the irritation of the geonim. Eventually, he became the head of the Jewish community. An expert also in philosophy and medicine, he became the family physician for a high vizier, whose many wives and children kept him busy.

Maimonides exemplified the intellectual model of the rabbi first put forth by Saadia. He wrote voluminously. His code of Jewish law summarized centuries of legal thought in simple rabbinic Hebrew and organized it in a new and rational manner; his medical treatises, written in Arabic, were studied by non-Jews; and his *Guide to the Perplexed*, also in Arabic, became one of the most famous books of medieval Jewish philosophy, expressing rather advanced ideas about religion in a veiled language that aroused suspicion in that very traditionalist age. The book became the focus of much controversy, especially when it was translated into Hebrew and was read by Jews in less sophisticated Christian lands who had less philosophical training.

The Jews of Palestine during the period of Muslim rule were less numerous and less outstanding than those of Egypt, Spain, and Iraq. The invading Arabs had taken away Jerusalem from the Byzantine empire in 638, and the conquerors revoked the prohibition—officially in effect since the time of Hadrian—against the Jews living there. For much of the Middle Ages, Palestine was governed by whatever Muslim power was in control of Egypt. It had a rabbinic academy of its own—at first in Tiberias, later in Ramla—that tried to contend for authority with the great academies of Iraq. But between Baghdad and Cairo, Palestine was merely a provincial territory for both Muslims and Jews.

Palestine became a focus of attention, though, when the crusaders arrived in 1099. For nearly two centuries, it was a war zone as Muslims defended it against the Christian knights who were trying—sometimes successfully—to wrest the holy Christian sites from the hands of those whom they regarded as infidels. Since the Jewish population of Palestine was

very small at this time, the Jews could only watch from the sidelines. A contemporaneous Hebrew poet in Spain, Judah Halevi, wrote poignantly of having to be a passive bystander looking on while Muslim and Christians contended over the Jewish holy city. Practically speaking, the Crusades had little immediate effect on the Jews of the Middle East, but in the long run, they were one contributing factor of many that led to the deterioration of the position of the Jews in Islamic lands.

The wars with the crusaders began a long process of demoralization that affected the Muslim world. Previously, Islam had seemed invincible: its rapid conquest of Persia and Byzantium in the seventh century, the immense extent of its empire, the vast wealth of its cities, and the fame of its scholars had all seemed miraculous. But Islamic power began to fray. The thirteenth century was the turning point. True, in 1291 the last crusaders were finally expelled from Palestine, but that was Islam's only success during the period, and it had taken two centuries to achieve it. By 1248, the Christian conquest of Spain—one of the jewels of Islam—was nearly

TOP: Three leaders of the First Crusade: Godfrey of Bouillon, Raymond of Toulouse, and Bohemund of Otranto, with his nephew Tancred.

ABOVE: The storming of Jerusalem in the First Crusade (1099) by Godfrey of Bouillon.

RIGHT: Battle between crusaders and Muslims at Ascalon (modern Ashkelon) in 1099. From a glass painting in the abbey of Saint-Denis.

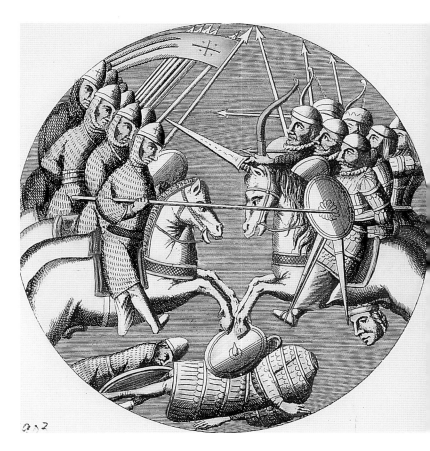

JUDAH HALEVI

Halevi was born in Tudela and grew up in a time of unrest, when the Christians were beginning to reconquer Spain from the Muslims. As a young man, he came to Granada, home to many famous Jewish intellectuals, courtiers, and poets, and quickly found a place among them, partly because of his quick wit and his ability to improvise poetry in Hebrew. He acquired an excellent rabbinic education and also studied philosophy and medicine; for many years, he lived as a respected doctor and as a pillar of the sophisticated Jewish community of Spain at the height of the Hebrew Golden Age. A prolific poet, he wrote sensual love poetry and elegant complimentary poems to his friends, many of whom were the great political and rabbinic leaders of the day.

But in middle age, Halevi's thoughts turned to piety. He wrote a book on religious thought called *The Kuzari*, which became very influential. He decided that, for all their religious feeling and Jewish loyalty, the Jewish leaders of Spain were not really living a life of service to God, but of service to man. He resolved to abandon his family and friends and make his way to the Holy Land to end his days as a pilgrim. When friends tried to dissuade him, he responded with lengthy poems defending his decision and expressing his determination to serve God alone.

My heart is in the East, and I am at the end
   of the West.
How can I taste my food, what pleasure does
   it bring?

He denounced Greek philosophy, which he thought encouraged people to rely on their own judgment rather than on the religious tradition, and he is even said to have sworn to stop writing poetry. In 1140, he set sail for Palestine.

But his resolution was not so easy to keep. Landing in Alexandria, he spent months visiting his acquaintances there, who entertained him lavishly and diverted his attention from his pilgrimage. He even went back to writing love poetry. At last, in the spring of 1141, he embarked on the last leg of his journey, and at this point we lose sight of him. All that is known is that he died during that summer; we do not know whether he reached his destination or if he died on the way.

Legend has supplied what history has not recorded. The story goes that Halevi arrived in the land of Israel and hastened to Jerusalem, where he threw himself on the ground to kiss the soil and to recite his "Ode to Zion." Just at the moment of the fulfillment of his vow, an Arab knight came along on his stallion and trampled him to death.

complete; Sicily had been conquered by the Normans; the coast of North Africa was under constant attack by Europeans; and, most significantly, the Mongols were on the march across Asia. In 1258, Baghdad was conquered and the caliphate extinguished. The Islamic Empire was no more. At the same time, Europe was awakening to mercantile life, with Italian city-states such as Venice, Pisa, and Genoa slowly becoming serious economic competitors of the Muslim states in the eastern Mediterranean. The whole world order was changing.

Islam responded by turning inward and expressing its anger against its non-Muslim subjects, both Christians and Jews. The laws regulating the behavior of dhimmis, often disregarded before, were now rigorously applied, so that Jews and Christians found themselves constantly harassed and humiliated. Both peoples had to wear distinguishing clothing and were prohibited from riding on donkeys within cities; churches and synagogues were vandalized; and Jewish physicians were prohibited from treating Muslim patients. As the economic power of the Muslim world declined in the fourteenth and fifteenth centuries, the conditions of non-Muslims deteriorated as well. Many converted to Islam. By 1481, the great city of Alexandria—one of the most important centers of Judaism since Hellenistic times—had only sixty Jewish families remaining.

But the oppression was not constant, there were no massacres, and there were others to share the burden (the Christians probably suffered even more from the deteriorating situation than did the Jews). For a brief period, after the Mongols conquered Baghdad, in 1258, there had even been a slight improvement of the Jewish condition, for the Mongols had not yet become Muslims and had no resentment toward Jews and Christians. But once the Mongols adopted Islam, they imposed the old Islamic dhimmi rules.

ABOVE: The Battle of Antioch, fought in 1098 during the First Crusade.

RIGHT: Arab battalions scattered by crusaders.

The deteriorating conditions of Jewish life left their mark in a decline in intellectual life as well. The splendid achievements of the period of the Islamic empire could not be matched in an atmosphere of intolerance and economic decline. Thus, Judaism in the Muslim territories stagnated.

The Jewish communities of northwest Africa did, however, fare somewhat better than those of other Muslim territories. In Tunisia and Algeria, after the Almohad fanaticism died down, the dhimmi rules were imposed with less rigor. When large numbers of Jews began fleeing Christian Spain in 1391 (see chapter five), they were welcome there. The community actually grew as a result and included some important writers and rabbis. In Morocco, the ruling family that established the Merinid dynasty (1286–1465) was less rigid in its religious attitudes than were most of their subjects, and these rulers

LEFT: Richard the Lion-Hearted leading crusaders in his victorious battle against the Muslims at Arsuf.

BELOW: A monk preaches to crusaders before the wall of Jerusalem.

permitted Jews to serve in the court at Fez. The populace, however, shared the negative feeling toward Jews that was common in the Muslim world at that time. After a number of riots, a special Jewish quarter, called *mellah*, was created (probably in 1438) for their protection. Riots and the subsequent establishment of mellahs became the pattern in Morocco ever after. Although the mellahs were originally intended as a protective gesture toward the Jews, the isolation felt like a kind of exile.

The second half of the fifteenth century completed the changes in the Middle East and in Jewish history that had been under way since the incursions of the crusaders into the Middle East. In 1453, the Ottoman Turks conquered Constantinople, putting an end to more than a thousand years of Byzantine history. The Ottomans proceeded to wipe out the decadent regimes in Palestine and Egypt, which they accomplished in 1517, and to gain control of Iraq and much of the Mediterranean coast of Africa, thus bringing to an end the age of Arab ascendency in the Middle East. In 1502, the Safavid dynasty gained control of Persia. By this time, the Jews had been expelled from Spain (1492) and from most of western Europe, as we shall see in the next chapter. The whole face of the Middle East had changed, and with it, the balance between the Jews of Islam and the Jews of Christendom.

The crusader fortress at Acre (modern Akko).

CHAPTER FIVE

THE JEWS OF MEDIEVAL CHRISTENDOM

THE EARLY HISTORY OF ASHKENAZIC JEWRY

*A*s we have seen, there was an important Jewish community in Rome in antiquity, but in the early Middle Ages there was an important community in the south of Italy as well. This territory was controlled by the Byzantine Empire, and the Byzantine Jews who found their way to it were closely attached to the declining Palestinian Jewish community. They established academies for the study of religious lore that acquired considerable fame, and the community prospered, despite occasional persecution by the Byzantine emperors.

In the ninth century, Jews from Italy began to migrate to the region around the Rhine, where Charlemagne (742–814) and his successors had established the capital of the Holy Roman Empire. The Frankish kings had already been encouraging the Jews to settle in the southern parts of present-day France. Charlemagne's son, Louis the Pious, as well as later emperors, urged the Jews to move into their northern territories, finding it advantageous to foster the growth of a community of businessmen and traders with international connections.

By the beginning of the eleventh century, the Jews had spread throughout what is now northern France, England, and Germany. Academies sprang up, especially in the Rhineland, and the foundations of Ashkenazic Jewry were laid. The term "Ashkenazic" refers to the Jews who descend from this original community of the Rhineland, a community that would spread during the Middle Ages

OPPOSITE: The old city of Jerusalem, with the wall from the Ottoman period in the foreground.

ABOVE: Charlemagne (742–814), king of the Franks, as painted by Albrecht Dürer around 1512.

to Poland and later to Russia, the United States, and Israel. In fact, their descendants form the dominant Jewish group in the United States today.

Despite the negative picture of the Jews that was taught by the Church, despite the Jews' status as outsiders, and despite occasional persecution, relations between Jews and the Christian populace had been mostly stable and benign for several centuries. But in the eleventh century, pressure began to mount for a crusade to capture the Holy Sepulchre from the Muslims. Emotional preachers inflamed the masses against the Muslims, and the rage spilled over onto the Jews, who the Church taught had actually killed Jesus. When the First Crusade began in 1096, its primary victims were the Jews of the Rhineland communities of Worms, Speyer, and Mainz. Though the local lords tried to protect the Jews, whom they were legally obligated to defend, the mobs could not be controlled, and there were widespread massacres and forced baptisms. Rather than fall into the hands of the crusaders and the mobs accompanying them, many Jews committed suicide, slaughtering their wives and children first. This wave of martyrdom left lasting scars on Ashkenazic Jewry. And there was more to come; the Second Crusade brought with it similar horrors, though some Jews were saved by the emperor Conrad III. In England, the Third Crusade was the occasion for mob riots against the Jews, and in 1190, the Jews of York killed themselves rather than fall into the hands of the crusaders.

Hostility between the populace and the Jews was constantly being renewed in western Europe. To the illiterate medieval European peasant, the Jews, with their odd customs, seemed to be not just outsiders, but devils or magicians performing harmful magic rites against man and God. Thus arose the blood libel, the accusation that the Jews require the blood of Christians for the performance of their religious rites, especially the rites of Passover. This libel plagued the Jews not only throughout the Middle Ages, but was revived as recently as 1911. The first case was apparently in Norwich, England, in 1144. In 1171, a Jew in Blois was accused of throwing the body of a Christian boy into the Loire; as a result, fifty Jews were burned alive. In 1181, three hundred Jews were killed near Vienna when three Christian boys disappeared. In 1255, the Jews of Lincoln were

TOP: The cathedral at Worms.

ABOVE: St. Bernard of Clairvaux (1090–1153) preaching to a group of crusaders at the outset of the Second Crusade in 1145.

accused of mutilating a child to use his intestines for witchcraft. Similar accusations were repeated constantly throughout Europe during this period, and entire Jewish communities were sometimes wiped out because of them.

Another libel that gained nearly universal credence in medieval Europe was that the Jews could not resist the temptation to torment Jesus and that they would satisfy this craving by obtaining communion wafers from the church and defiling them. Although kings and the higher clergy did often try to defend the Jews against superstitious ideas, the unlettered lower clergy were frequently responsible for inciting the crowds with such accusations. Despite all the discrimination that Jews had to bear in the lands of Islam, such barbarism was unheard of in those sophisticated territories during this period.

The increasing marginalization of the Jews was due in part to their economic situation. At the time, European life was governed by the feudal system, according to which most people were attached to the land and owed loyalty and military service to a lord. But the Jews, originally brought in for the sake of commerce, were outside this system. They owed their loyalty to kings, princes, or bishops who had invited them into their realms. Occupied mainly in

trade, the Jews tended to live in towns, not on feudal estates. Thus, they would have been clearly marked as outsiders by their social status alone regardless of their religious beliefs and exotic rituals. As townspeople, some Jews might have been attracted to crafts; but crafts came to be increasingly dominated by guilds, which admitted only Christians.

The Jewish position in Christian Europe weakened further with the elevation of Innocent III to the papacy in 1198. With the Church being the dominant political force in Europe, Innocent waged war on religious dissenters. His persecution of the

RIGHT: The Altneuschul, a medieval synagogue in Prague, built in 1270 and still standing.

BELOW: Crusaders setting sail for Palestine.

heretical Christian Albigensian sect in what is now southern France led to the founding of the Inquisition, which would play an important role in Spain and Portugal in the fifteenth and sixteenth centuries. Innocent enforced the old policy of attempting to reduce the Jews to a minimal existence. The summit was reached in 1215 at the Fourth Lateran Council—convened by Innocent—which forbade the Jews to practice any Christian occupation, to employ Christians, or even to associate with Christians. It also created the hated Jewish badge (a patch that Jews had to wear on their clothing so that they might be easily distinguished from Christians). Jews were systematically driven out of trades and reduced to the bottom of society, able to survive only as peddlers, pawnbrokers, and traders in secondhand objects.

The Council did inadvertently create one new sphere of economic activity for Jews, though, by prohibiting Christians from usury. Here was a practice that was absolutely essential for commercial growth and that could not be conducted by the majority population: it was the perfect field for the pariah people, and would make them despised for centuries.

In addition to the measures designed to undermine the Jewish community economically, the thirteenth century also saw systematic efforts to under-

Pope Innocent III (1198–1216), persecutor of the Albigensians, founder of the Inquisition in southern France, and author of restrictive legislation against the Jews.

TOP: A Jewish moneylender, as depicted in a fifteenth-century woodcut.

ABOVE: A Jewish scholar, as depicted in a fifteenth-century woodcut.

mine Judaism as a religion. In 1232, the books of Maimonides were burned in southern France. The Talmud itself was put on trial—at the instigation of a Jewish apostate—in 1240 in Paris, and all available copies were burned.

The ruin of the Jews in England began in 1275, when Edward I deprived them of moneylending as a livelihood, declaring all debts to Jews void. After imprisoning the leaders of the community and demanding a huge ransom for them, he finally put an end to the history of the Jews of medieval England by banishing all Jews from his realm in 1290. The Jews were not readmitted officially until four centuries had passed.

Following Edward's example, Philip the Fair of France seized all Jewish property and expelled all Jews from his country in 1306. Although the Jews were permitted to return under the following reign, disaster awaited them. In 1320, the mob known as the Shepherd's Crusade destroyed 120 Jewish communities, and in the following year, five thousand Jews were burned alive on the accusation of having poisoned the wells. By 1322, there were hardly any Jews left in all of France.

Then in 1348 the Black Death swept through Europe causing disaster without regard to religion or historical origin. A third of the entire population of Europe—Christians and Jews alike—was wiped out. Seized with hysteria, the populace turned to extreme religious fervor to express and allay their fear. Soon the rumor began that the Jews had caused the plague by poisoning the wells, and a systematic execution began. The pope's attempt to intervene against this absurdity was unavailing in the face of mass hysteria. One after another, the Jewish communities of western Europe, especially in the various German territories, were rounded up and burned.

In the ensuing decades, the Jews who had fled filtered back to France and Germany, but in miserable condition and to an unstable life. They were definitively expelled from France in 1394, and during the course of the fifteenth century, they were definitively expelled from the various German states of central

Europe. At the end of the fifteenth century came the expulsion from Spain. But that is a story that deserves to be told separately.

At the eastern end of Europe, the Byzantine Empire continued the harsh policies toward the Jews set in motion by Constantine and interrupted by a brief respite under Julian the Apostate only to be revived by Justinian I. By the time of the Muslim conquests, the Jews of the Byzantine Empire were in despair over their persecution by the emperor Heraclius, whom the Jews saw as an evil figure of Satanic proportions.

The Muslim conquest of Byzantine Palestine and Egypt did not benefit their brethren in the Byzantine heartlands in southeastern Europe and western Asia. Here, there was no relief from restrictive legislation and periodic persecutions. This

Illuminated manuscript Bible from Provence, c. 1422. This is the first page of Genesis, with the word meaning "in the beginning" prominently featured.

oppression extended as well to southern Italy, a Byzantine province with an important Jewish community (see the beginning of this chapter). The most important persecution was during the reign of the emperor Basil I, who in 873–74 ordered the forced conversion of the Jews; the decree was revived by Romanus I Lecapenus in 943.

Some of the persecuted Jews of Byzantine Italy found refuge by fleeing to Khazaria. This kingdom, located in the Caucasus and adjacent areas that today are in southern Ukraine, was itself a remarkable phenomenon. Though the Jews were everywhere a subject people, and in much of the world persecuted as well, Khazaria was the one place in the medieval world where the Jews actually were their own masters. It was founded by the Khazars, a Turkic people who had migrated from central Asia and whose rulers had adopted Judaism in the early eighth century. Though Jewish by religion, they remained somewhat apart from mainstream Jewish institutions. But their existence was known in the Jewish world, and occasional contact was made between them and mainstream Jewish leaders like Hasdai Ibn Shaprut of Spain, who corresponded with Joseph, the Khazar king in the tenth century. To the oppressed Jews of the world, the Khazars were a source of pride and hope, for their existence seemed to prove that God had not completely abandoned His people.

CHRISTIAN SPAIN

We have already seen how the Gothic kings of Spain attempted to eliminate Judaism in the seventh century and that the Jews were saved by the arrival of the Muslim conquerors in the eighth century. Under Islam, Spain had become the most populous—and most successful—Jewish community in Europe.

Most of Spain remained under Muslim control until the eleventh century, though the area around Barcelona quickly reverted to the Christians. When the Castilian king Alfonso VI succeeded in conquering Toledo from the Muslims in 1085, the first

Some Famous Ashkenazic Rabbis

Rabbi Gershom

Rabbi Gershom, the Light of the Exile (960–1028), lived in Mainz (in what is now Germany), where his tombstone survived World War II. He was one of the founders of the Ashkenazic tradition of rabbinic scholarship. He was famous for his enactments, which are still considered by religious Ashkenazic Jews to have the force of law. These include the prohibition of polygamy; of reading letters addressed to others; of reminding Jews who were forcibly converted to Christianity and then returned to their people of things they did while outside the community; and of divorcing a wife against her will. He also composed important liturgical poems.

Rashi

Rashi (1040–1104), who was educated at Worms and taught in Troyes (France), made a living as a vintner. He is venerated by all students of the Jewish tradition because of two works. The first is his commentary on the Torah, a popular work in simple Hebrew that is actually a summary of the most common rabbinic opinions of the meaning of Scripture. It is replete with legendary material, and is studied weekly by ordinary religious Jews worldwide. The second is his commentary on the Babylonian Talmud, also a work of extreme popularity, which explains the eliptical text of the Talmud by filling in the gaps in the exposition, making it possible for ordinary people to figure out the meaning of the Talmud without a teacher to guide them.

Rabbenu Tam

Rabbenu Tam (c. 1100–71) was a grandson of Rashi; he lived in Ramerupt (France) by viticulture and moneylending. During the Second Crusade, he was attacked by crusaders, but somehow survived. He was regarded as the most authoritative decisor of Jewish law among Ashkenazic Jews in his time, but his opinions were regarded highly even by some Sephardic and Italian rabbis. His annotations to the Babylonian Talmud are the basis of the Tosafot, anonymous brief discussions of talmudic passages that, since the beginning of the age of printing, have always appeared together with Rashi's commentary. He engaged in debates on Hebrew grammar that were current among Spanish Jews, and wrote some poetry in the metric system pioneered by them, probably thanks to the influence of Abraham Ibn Ezra.

major step in the Christian conquest of Spain, he extended hospitality to Andalusian Jews, and Christian Spain became a haven for them during the Almohad persecution (see chapter four). Thus, the foundation was laid for the beginning of a new Jewish community in Christian Spain, and soon Jewish courtiers, administrators, and financiers were occupying similar positions to those that Jews had once held in Muslim Spain. These Jews were particularly useful to the Christian kingdoms because they knew the land and how to administer it; and most important, they knew the language of the land, which was still Arabic. Yet there was no fear that they might subvert Christian rule as there might have been for captured Muslims pressed into government service.

By 1248, all of Spain was controlled by the Christian kingdoms except for one remaining Muslim enclave, the territory of Granada. Arabic still had great prestige as the language of high culture and the key to Greek philosophy, since the ancient writings were only available in Arabic translation. Because of its unique mixture of Arab, Jewish, and Christian scholars, Spain became a center for the transmission of science and philosophy to Europe. Jews collaborated with monks in translating Greek writings from Arabic into Latin, often by way of Hebrew versions.

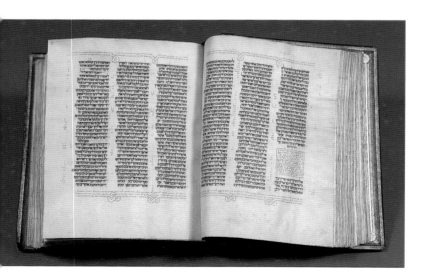

A Bible manuscript open to the end of Numbers. The marginal notes in red are known as Masoretic notes.

This work was especially encouraged by Alfonso X of Castile, known as Alfonso the Wise (r. 1252–84). From all over Europe, Christian scholars streamed into Toledo to acquire the new translations, which were a stimulus to the revival of learning throughout Europe, as well as a harbinger of the Renaissance. Alfonso X had Jewish courtiers in his entourage and Jewish scientists—especially astronomers—as advisers for his many cultural projects.

The situation in Aragon was somewhat less favorable. Barcelona, and northeastern Spain in general, had been an important Jewish community; its geographical and political ties to southern France made it a bridge between Ashkenazic Jewry and Spanish Jewry, whose individual characters differed from one another as much as Spain itself differed from the rest of western Europe. Moreover, in the thirteenth century, there was an important religious academy in Gerona. Not only the Talmud was studied there, but also the kabbala, the new wave of Jewish mysticism that had originated in Provence. (This system of religious thought would receive its definitive formulation in the thirteenth-century work called the Zohar, by Moses de Leon, a Castilian rabbi.) But James I of Aragon came under pressure to induce the Jews to convert. In 1263, he held a disputation, intended to demonstrate to the Jews the error of their ways. Christianity was represented by an apostate named Pablo Christiani and a team of monks. To represent Judaism, James summoned the reluctant Rabbi Moses ben Nahman, one of the great Talmudists and mystics of the Middle Ages. The rabbi handled himself with acumen and tact, but when the debate was over, he had to flee for his life. He spent his last years in Jerusalem.

The next century saw the liberal atmosphere that had existed in Castile dissipate. With the end of the transitional period of the conquest and the development of a Spanish culture based on Romance languages, the Jews seemed more like a vestige of the earlier pre-Christian period and were therefore perceived more and more as outsiders. Even the enlighted Alfonso X had included harsh provisions

The skyline of modern Toledo, Spain.

for governing the Jews in the law code he established; toward the end of his reign, he imprisoned his Jewish advisers, killed several of them, and brought the great Jewish community of Toledo to the point of utter ruin. After his reign, the situation of the Jews declined even further.

The deteriorating attitude of the Church toward the Jews, as expressed in the Fourth Lateran Council and the increased circulation of preaching monks, gradually contributed to the negative atmosphere surrounding the Jews in Spain. And like the rest of Europe, Spain blamed the Jews for the suffering incurred during the Black Death of 1348.

In 1391, intensified anti-Jewish preaching led to an attack on the Jewish community of Seville, and the fever spread to other Spanish cities. Thousands of Jews were killed and many fled, swelling those communities in North Africa that had rulers who were favorably disposed to Jews, as we have seen in chapter four. But the most unusual development was the mass conversion to Christianity, something unprecedented in Jewish history.

Jewish Spain now entered into the terrible fifteenth century, during which the constant pressure to convert created a third community alongside the Christans and Jews: the *conversos*. These people, who became ever more numerous, were Christian in their behavior. Many were sincere in their Christian convictions, but others converted only to escape persecution and continued to think of themselves as Jews. Even among those who really thought of themselves as Christians, there were many who continued to practice some Jewish rituals—out of habit, loyalty, or superstition; and most continued to stay in contact with their friends and relatives who had not converted.

Some of the converts to Christianity enjoyed considerable success in the Church. Rabbi Solomon Halevi of Burgos entered a career as a cardinal under the name Paul of Burgos. A convert, Joshua of Lorca, now known as Geronimo de Santa Fe, persuaded Ferdinand I of Aragon to hold the infamous Tortosa dispute; for a whole year, the chief rabbis and leaders of Aragonese Jewry were harangued by Geronimo and others to the effect that the Messiah had already come and that the Jews were adhering to their old ways out of sheer wickedness. Unlike the debate that had been held under the auspices of James I in the time of Moses ben Nahman, this argument was conducted under rules that severely restricted the Jews in what they were allowed to say by way of reply. By the time the "debate" was over, some of the Jewish spokesmen yielded and converted to Christianity, with a demoralizing effect on the entire Jewish community.

Gradually, the focus of attention shifted from the dwindling, increasingly impoverished, and less visible Jewish community to the growing and ever more influential conversos. New Christians were everywhere, contending for positions in society, court, and the Church that had been closed to them when they were Jews. They were accused of having converted only in order to advance themselves and to take control of the country; those who retained some vestigial Jewish observances were accused of being insincere converts. By the end of the century, thousands of third-generation Christians who had never known any other religion and who had all but forgotten their Jewish origin were still thought of as "New Christians"; because of their distant background, they suffered contempt and discrimination.

The final chapter for Spanish Jewry began when the two Spanish kingdoms were united upon the marriage of Ferdinand of Aragon and Isabella of Castile in 1469. Determined to complete the conquest and Christianization of Spain, they devoted years and vast treasures to conquering the tiny kingdom of Granada, the last Muslim outpost on the peninsula. Isabella, in particular, was determined to purify Spanish Christianity, and for this purpose, she received permission from Pope Sixtus IV to introduce the Inquisition into Spain.

The Spanish Inquisition began in 1480; it was later extended to Portugal, where it would continue, unbelievable as it may seem, until 1820. It was extended to the Spanish territories in the Americas as well. People would be denounced anonymously to the Inquisition on suspicion of observing some Jewish traditions or not being sufficiently punctilious in Christian observances. In response, the accused was examined under torture. Those who confessed were expected to denounce relatives and friends. The property of the convicted—and often of the merely accused—was confiscated. While uncon-

Ferdinand, king of Aragon (1452–1516) and Isabella, queen of Castile (1451–1504). Their marriage, in 1469, joined the two largest kingdoms of the Iberian peninsula, in effect creating Spain.

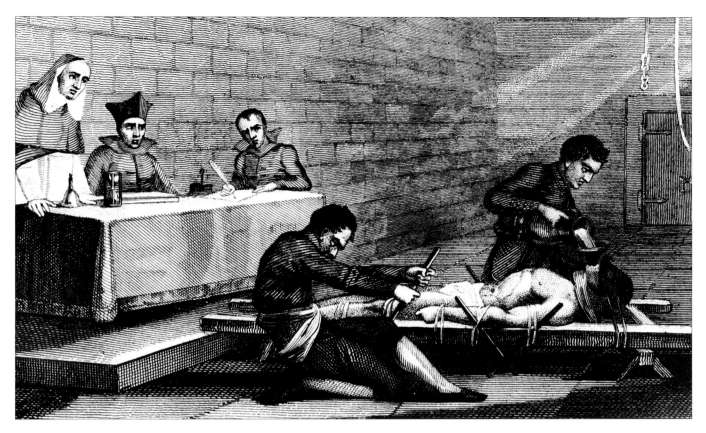

ABOVE: The Inquisition at work. Two men torture the accused, while the inquisitors wait for a confession.

BELOW: Columbus Received by Ferdinand and Isabella, by E. Deveira.

fessed and unrepentant heretics were burned alive, the repentant were strangled before being burned. So that the Church would not actually have to spill blood, the executions were carried out by the state. These executions were generally performed at a public ceremony known as an auto-da-fé, a huge spectacle put on for the masses in the presence of assembled royalty and clergy.

Contrary to the impression held by many people, the Inquisition did not concern itself with Jews; after all, following the expulsion of 1492, there were not officially supposed to be any Jews in Spain. It was empowered only to detect heresy among Christians, and in particular to look for signs of Judaizing among the conversos. But the sufferings of the conversos are a part of Jewish history, because the persecution of the Jews had created the problem in the first place and because for centuries, many of the conversos' descendants would be haunted by family traditions and memories linking them with Judaism. Some of these descendants would eventually leave

Blood Libel

One of the most persistent reasons for persecuting the Jews has been the widespread belief that they are in the habit of murdering non-Jews in order to use their blood for religious rituals, especially Passover. This libel is connected with the broader view that Jews are not truly human but are actually monsters connected with the devil, who employ special rites and subterfuges in order to appear like other men. The belief that Jews sacrifice non-Jews in their rituals goes back to Hellenistic times. When Christians were a small minority in the pagan world, they, too, were sometimes accused of having such rituals. But the blood libel came to be widespread and exclusively connected to the Jews in medieval Christian Europe, where the Jews were felt to be outsiders and where their rituals were considered exotic and suspicious. The first full-fledged accusation was made against the Jews of Norwich (England), in 1144, when it was alleged that the Jews seized a Christian child named William before Easter, tortured him as Jesus had been tortured, and hanged him on Good Friday. Other important occurrences were in Gloucester in 1168; Blois in 1171; Saragossa in 1182; Fulda (Germany) in 1235; Lincoln (England) in 1255; and Munich in 1286. This last is mentioned by Chaucer in the *Canterbury Tales*, in connection with a fictional tale of his own about a blood libel. In addition to using Christian blood for ritual purposes, Jews were accused of drinking it or using it as a cure for the operation of circumcision, as an aphrodisiac, or as an ingredient in sorcery. Perhaps the most bizarre of these claims was connected with the widespread notion that Jewish men menstruate like women; according to some Christians, by drinking Christian blood, Jewish men were able to halt the humiliating flow of menstrual blood.

Although sophisticated Christians did not give credence to the blood libel—it was rejected even by Pope Innocent IV—it was so widespread that a commission of inquiry was established by Holy Roman Emperor Frederick II. In their report, the commissioners quite correctly pointed to the scrupulous avoidance of blood by Jews in their dietary regulations as evidence that Jews could not possibly use human blood for religious rites or any other purpose. But the blood libel has never disappeared. It was revived as part of the anti-Semitic government politics of late czarist Russia, when a Jew named Mendel Beilis was charged with the ritual killing of a Christian child. Beilis was jailed for two years, but he was acquitted when he finally went to trial in 1913. The police who investigated the case had determined almost immediately that the child had been killed by a gang of criminals, but their information was suppressed because the minister of justice insisted on treating the case as a ritual murder charge.

the Iberian peninsula and attempt to rejoin the Jewish people, even after their families had been Christian for centuries.

During the initial part of this period of horrors, the rulers continued to employ Jews; two rabbis, Don Isaac Abravanel and Don Abraham Senior, were among the inner circle of courtiers of the Catholic monarchs. But early in 1492, when Granada surrendered, the Catholic monarchs decided to complete the religious unification of the peninsula by expelling the Jews. The edict of expulsion was signed on March 31, ordering the Jews to leave by the end of July. With that stroke, the greatest medieval Jewish community was destroyed. It was not long before

Portugal followed suit, leaving the entire Iberian peninsula officially free of Jews.

The culture of the Jews of Spain differed in many ways from that of the Jews elsewhere in medieval Europe. The tradition of the Judeo-Arabic Golden Age was part of their historical memory. Until the fourteenth century, they had been much better integrated into the larger society than had the Ashkenazic Jews. In short, the Spanish Jews thought of themselves as a distinct community of Jews, and to this day their descendants are known as Sephardim, from the Hebrew word for Spain. In the next chapter, we shall follow the fortunes of the Sephardic community after its expulsion from Spain.

Deputation of Jews before Ferdinand and Isabella. Engraving after a painting by Alonzo Chaappel. On the right, Torquemada, Isabella's confessor, admonishes her not to relent from her decision to expel the Jews.

CHAPTER SIX

THE JEWS IN THE ISLAMIC WORLD, PART II (1453–1948)

While the Jews of Spain were undergoing the traumas of the fifteenth century, changes were occurring in the eastern Mediterranean that would lay the foundations for their salvation as a community. Having conquered Constantinople in 1453, the Turkish Ottoman empire embarked on the conquest of the central Muslim lands, injecting new life into the moribund Middle East. For one and a half centuries, the Ottoman empire would be a major antagonist of Europe, where the modern states were just coming into being. As an expanding nation consisting mostly of military and agricultural people, the Ottoman empire considered the Jewish exiles from Spain, with their commercial skills and international connections, to be an economic asset. Sultan Bayazid II is said to have welcomed the exiles, expressing incredulity that Ferdinand of Aragon had expelled such industrious and useful subjects.

At this stage, the Ottomans were not religiously dogmatic and did not enforce the humiliating restrictions that had formerly been so oppressive. Paying the special dhimmi taxes, the non-Muslims were generally left alone, except for occasional local mistreatment.

OPPOSITE: Constantinople at the height of the Ottoman Empire, as depicted by the painter F. Herink.

LEFT: Sixteenth-century miniature showing Constantinople when it was taken by Mehmet II the Conqueror.

ABOVE: Sixteenth-century miniature depicting Ottoman troops conquering a city.

PERSONALITIES:
ISAAC LURIA AND THE MYSTICS OF SAFED

Isaac Luria (1534–72) was a rabbi and mystic who lived and taught in the Galilean town of Safed during the sixteenth century, when the town flourished as a center for Jewish mysticism. He was the central figure among the many famous and influential rabbis of that age and place. Although most of the Jewish population of Palestine consisted of Sephardim whose ancestors had fled Spain in 1492, Luria was Ashkenazic. He was therefore called Rabbi Isaac the Ashkenazi, which yielded the Hebrew acronym "Ari," or "The Lion," and it is by this title that he is generally known. Others explain the title as deriving from the Hebrew words for "Rabbi Isaac the Divine." His disciples were called "The Lion's Whelps."

The Ari, like many Jewish mystics of the period, was not only a mystic, but also a specialist in religious law, a field that might seem quite opposed in its dryness and pedantry to the mystic's intellectual and imaginary freedom and emotionalism. But to Jewish mystics, these approaches were not considered to be opposed. The intense study of the law produced not only technical advances but also a kind of intellectual ecstasy; furthermore, even the finest details of legal reasoning were invested with mystical meaning.

Thus, Rabbi Joseph Caro, an older contemporary of the Ari who also lived in Safed, composed commentaries on texts of religious law unparalleled in their detail, and legal codes unparalleled in their authority (he was the author of *The Prepared Table*, mentioned in this chapter). But as a mystic, he also believed that the Mishnah (see chapter three) appeared to him regularly in his dreams in the form of a woman to give him spiritual guidance and intellectual insight.

The mystics of Safed in the sixteenth century had a significant influence on the practice of Judaism in later generations. They devised new religious rituals that found their way into the prayer books of nearly all Jewish communities. Their graves are still objects of pilgrimage by religious Jews, especially for Jews from the Middle East. The two synagogues in which the Ari preached still stand in Safed, and can be visited to this day.

The prestige of Spanish Jewish culture and the Iberian pride of the Spanish Jews were such that these people quickly came to dominate the Jewish communities in which they arrived, sweeping away from before them local customs and carrying with them their Spanish language and folkways. Important Spanish-speaking Jewish communities sprang up in Constantinople, Salonica, Edirne, Smyrna, and many other cities. These communities were continually augmented as Marranos (as the conversos were generally called in vulgar Spanish— the word means "pigs") fled the Inquisition in the course of the following century. But not all the newcomers were Sephardim, for the Ottoman empire was attractive also to Jews from Italy and Europe.

While in Spain, the Jews had spoken the same language as their neighbors, though they did use some Hebrew terms referring to Jewish customs and some distinctively Jewish locutions. When they were exiled and came to the Ottoman empire, these Jews retained the language they had spoken in Spain, feeling themselves culturally superior to the local Jews whose communities they now joined. Thus, the Spanish Jews formed a distinct linguistic community within the Ottoman empire. In this they were not alone, for subjects of the empire included many national, religious, and linguistic groups; in a metropolis like Constantinople that included Armenian, Greek, and other communities alongside the Turks, the Jews did not stand out especially on linguistic grounds. The Spanish spoken by the Jewish exiles came to be known as "Judezmo" (Jewish) or "Ladino" (Latin), and it is still used today by an ever-diminishing number of speakers.

Jewish businessmen quickly rose to public prominence in the Ottoman empire, encouraged by the sultans who were anxious to increase the empire's economic power. By the middle of the sixteenth century, many individual Jews had risen to positions of power and influence as doctors, financiers, and even as statesmen. During the first century of Ottoman exile, the Spanish Jewish grandees succeeded in reestablishing the pattern of court Jews that had existed in Spain in both its Muslim and Christian phases.

The masses of Jewish refugees from Spain reached not only the heartland of the Ottoman empire, but its provinces as well. When the Ottomans conquered Palestine and Egypt in 1517, this impoverished and wretched community received an influx of energetic refugees from a more advanced cultural and material environment. With the new refugees, new communities sprang to life. The most important of these communities was Safed, a Galilean town that hitherto had not played a prominent role in history;

A sixteenth-century depiction of Jerusalem, drawn in Cologne.

The Battle of Lepanto in 1571, in which a coalition of European states defeated the Turks.

After leaving Portugal with his aunt, João studied at the university in Louvain and then joined his family's business in Antwerp. His business connections put him in contact with some of the most powerful people of Europe, such as Emperor Charles V, the future Emperor Maximilian, and the French king Francis I. When his aunt was turned over to the Inquisition, João was able to secure her release thanks to his connections with the Turkish government, which was in a position to put pressure on the Spanish. Doña Gracia then moved to Ferrara, where she returned openly to Judaism, finally settling in Constantinople in 1553. The next year, João joined her there and also reverted to Judaism under the name Joseph Nasi.

Ever since her departure from Portugal, Doña Gracia had actively supported efforts to aid the flight of the Marranos and to put a stop to the Inquisition in Portugal. In Constantinople she continued this activity, and made a point of patronizing scholars and established Jewish religious institutions. Her power was such that in 1556–57 she tried to organize a boycott to punish the city of Ancona for burning twenty-six Marranos. Don Joseph joined her in these activities, trying to get the city of Venice to make one of its islands a refuge for Marranos.

Don Joseph also supported the Ottoman prince Selim in his struggle for the throne against his brother Bayazid, in return for which Selim rewarded him with lofty titles and extensive powers. After coming to the throne in 1566, Selim appointed Joseph duke of the island of Naxos and later count of Andros. In 1561, Joseph became, in effect, lord of Tiberias and the environs. He rebuilt the town as a center for the manufacture of wool and silk, hoping to benefit both the local economy and that of the empire. For this purpose, he had mulberry trees planted and Italian Jewish refugees brought in as workers. Though the experiment did not take, it did contribute to the town's brief flourishing.

It is not clear whether what Don Joseph had in mind for Tiberias was merely economic development or the beginning of a Jewish resettlement of

Jerusalem, Gaza, Hebron, Acre, and Tiberias also prospered. In fact, Tiberias entered into an especially auspicious time when it was given as a gift to Don Joseph Nasi (1524–79), the most spectacular of the Jewish grandees of the Ottoman empire.

Don Joseph Nasi was the nephew of the equally spectacular Doña Gracia Nasi (c. 1510–69). Born in Portugal, Doña Gracia came from a family of prominent Spanish Jews who had probably fled there in 1492. When Judaism was outlawed in Portugal in 1497, the family became Marranos. After the death of her husband, a Marrano with business connections in Antwerp, Doña Gracia took her family, including her nephew—known at that time as João, the son of a royal physician—to England, the Low Countries, and Venice, where her own sister denounced her as a Judaizer.

Palestine. When the Turks went to war with Venice over Cyprus, he was promised the kingship of the island, and here, too, he may have had thoughts of turning it into a political solution to the Marrano problem. But after the Turkish defeat at Lepanto (1571), Don Joseph's influence waned and his career went into decline.

Safed, the largest city of Palestine during this period, became an important intellectual center. The century following the upheaval of 1492 saw an intensification of mystical religious thought, and many of the pietistic Jews were drawn to its acade-mies. Here, the central figure was Rabbi Isaac Luria (known as the Ari), who developed a revised approach to the great mystical classic of Spain, the Zohar. His ideas were spread by his disciples to all parts of the Ottoman empire and from there to Italy and Europe. Many rituals of his devising were adopted even by Jews who were not adherents of his mystical system. One of his most important colleagues was Rabbi Joseph Caro, a mystic and legal thinker, whose book *The Prepared Table*, published in 1564–65, remains the last great codification of Jewish law.

Joseph Caro (1488–1575), the great mystic and codifier of religious law, with a page from *The Prepared Table*, his definitive code of Jewish law. Only the twelve lines printed in square letters just above the center of the page are from the text of Caro's code; everything else on the page is commentary by later rabbis.

Another manifestation of the unrest caused by the expulsion from Spain was a series of messianic movements. One colorful figure was an imposter named David Reubeni, who claimed to be a prince from a Jewish kingdom in Ethiopia bearing a mission to liberate the Holy Land from the Turks. He managed to get an interview with the pope and an introduction to the king of Portugal, but he was imprisoned and shipped to Spain, where he probably died in an auto-da-fé. His disciple, Solomon Molcho, a Marrano, settled in Safed and declared 1540 as the year of the messianic redemption. But the Messiah did not appear, and Solomon was burned at the stake by the Inquisition in Mantua.

The most influential of the messianic movements arose in the seventeenth century. Shabbetai Zevi,

Shabbetai Zevi, the pseudo-Messiah, as sketched from life in 1666.

born in Smyrna in 1626, was a mystic who came to the conviction that he was the Messiah. After acquiring some followers, he declared himself as such publicly by pronouncing the ineffable name of God. As a result, he was promptly excommunicated. He then traveled to Constantinople, Salonica, Cairo, and Jerusalem, gathering adherents. The most important of these was the mysterious Nathan of Gaza, who was really responsible for organizing Shabbetai Zevi's followers into the mass movement called Sabbateanism. When Zevi returned to Smyrna in 1665, he was acclaimed by multitudes who believed his prediction that 1666 would be the messianic year; this claim was taken seriously by European Jews as well. But when he traveled to Constantinople for the dethronement of the sultan, which was to be the opening event of the messianic age, he was arrested and imprisoned. The fortress in which he was held became the object of pilgrimage for hundreds, and his followers awaited his signal to begin the journey to the Holy Land. But the moment never came, for, confronted with an ultimatum by the sultan, Shabbetai Zevi converted to Islam, taking the name Mehmet Effendi.

The collapse of Shabbetai's pretensions came as a demoralizing blow to many Jewish communities, not all of them in the Ottoman ambit. Many in Italy, Poland, and Lithuania, as well as in the empire, refused to give up hope that all would turn out well, telling themselves that his conversion was merely a ruse or a temporary setback. Nathan of Gaza himself maintained that Shabbetai had gone into hiding in some higher sphere, whence he would eventually return in triumph. In the eighteenth century, Jacob Frank revived the movement in Poland, calling himself an incarnation of Shabbetai Zevi and introducing a bizarre blend of kabbalistic, Christian, Muslim, and Jewish—mainly Zoharic—doctrines. But the overall effect of the collapse of the Sabbatean movement was the collapse of morale throughout the Jewish world and the retreat from general intellectual activity. More and more, Jews worldwide limited their scope to the conscientious observance of

Jewish law and to living insular lives within their own communities.

For the Jews of the Ottoman empire, this deflation corresponded to the general economic and cultural decline of the age. The inherent weaknesses of the once-proud Ottoman empire began to show themselves as early as the end of the sixteenth century, when the central government began to lose its control over the provinces. The Jewish courtiers of the seventeenth century no longer maintained the stature of their predecessors in the age of the Nasis. In general, the seventeenth century saw a tendency toward religious conservatism and an emphasis on the Islamic character of the society. Little by little, the laws of discrimination were reintroduced, and Jews again were required to wear distinctive clothing. One sultan raised money by threatening to kill all the Jews of the realm and then accepting a bribe to revoke the decree. Regulations governing the number and construction of synagogues were again enforced. Thus, the Jews of the empire developed the custom of praying in private homes; this explains the fact that many small synagogues throughout the Middle East are named after individuals or families. The situation remained grim through the seventeenth and eighteenth centuries, and into the nineteenth, as the economy stagnated and most people, including the Jews, were reduced to poverty.

While Europe was experiencing the great flowering that had begun around 1500, progress in the Middle East came to a halt, until Napoleon's arrival in Egypt in 1798. European powers had long had commercial interests in the Ottoman territories, but the military interventions of France and, slightly later, of England, changed the whole face of the region. The chief beneficiaries of Europeanization in the region were the dhimmis.

During the nineteenth century, European powers made arrangements with their governments to protect their Christian trading partners. Ottoman foreign trade had generally been in the hands of dhimmis, especially Greeks and Armenians, and there still were some wealthy Jewish traders among the

Napoleon Bonaparte in Cairo, which he conquered in 1798.

wretched Jewish masses. Since Islamic law did not distinguish one kind of dhimmi from another, the Jewish traders benefitted from the European protection along with Christians.

But indirect European influence worked even more effectively to the benefit of the Jews. As part of a larger plan to reinvigorate and modernize the failing empire, the sultan promulgated a series of reforms, including the granting of full civil equality to non-Muslims, in 1839. Influenced by political ideas emanating from France, this move was a radical change, for up until this point a person's status in

A *shiviti*, a marker hung on an eastern wall in traditional Jewish homes to mark the proper direction for prayer. They are often beautifully designed, like this one, made in Istanbul in 1838–39 by Moses Ganbash.

Muslim states had been determined by religion; there was no concept of citizenship. Years passed before this reform actually took effect, and in the empire's Arab provinces, where the empire's grip was no longer firm, the decree went completely unnoticed and unenforced.

Further edicts were soon issued. In 1856, it was decreed that non-Muslims could no longer be referred to abusively in official documents. More important, religious communities were now organized into the millet system, in which each non-Muslim religious community became an officially recognized autonomous body whose members were represented to the state through designated communal leaders. Thus, the Jews and other dhimmis made progress—officially, at least—toward political and legal equality as well as official recognition.

Under European pressure, similar regulations were introduced in Tunisia and Egypt—both of which were autonomous provinces of the empire with large Jewish populations—though the Jews did not achieve full civil equality in Egypt until 1882,

French colonial troops from Algeria on the western front.

after the British occupation. French rule in Algeria also improved the Jews' lot. But in Morocco, despite being pressured by the British, leaders refused to introduce similar reforms.

The same Western influences that brought ideas of civil equality to the Middle East, though, also brought Christian anti-Semitism. The Muslims of the Middle East may have held non-Muslims in contempt and treated them uncivilly, but intensive contact with Christian Europe now taught them the mythology of anti-Semitism that had become traditional, even self-evident, in medieval Europe.

With all the discrimination suffered by the Jews in the Muslim world, it was not until 1840, with the Damascus affair, that the first serious blood libel occurred there. This case, in which a Jewish barber was accused of killing an Italian monk and his servant in order to use their blood for Passover, touched off an international scandal. Several Jews were tortured and killed, and riots were touched off throughout the Middle East in which Muslims joined the Christians in attacking Jews. The French supported the Christians, while England and Austria tried to intervene on behalf of the Jews. Of course, the background of these interventions was the rivalry of the colonial powers for economic and political influence in the Levant in the eastern Mediterranean. The blood libel was renewed repeatedly throughout the region.

In 1860, an international Jewish organization, the Alliance Israélite Universelle, was founded in Paris for the purpose of working for the emancipation and welfare of Jews worldwide. Throughout the Ottoman empire and North Africa, this group established schools that offered religious and secular education in Hebrew and French. These schools produced a class of Westernized Middle Eastern Jews, who had the same advantage over the non-Westernized and barely educated Muslim masses as did the Christians, who attended missionary schools established by various denominations throughout the Middle East.

While this process of education and liberation afforded the Jews and Christians great economic advantages, it was bitterly resented by the Muslim majority, who, largely limited to their own cultural world and their traditional poverty, had to watch the Jews and Christians become disproportionately wealthy and powerful. As a result, the improvement of the Middle Eastern Jews' legal and economic position ironically led to the deterioration of their actual social position and physical security. Furthermore, most of the Arab lands, except for Egypt, suffered from a general collapse of the rule of law during the nineteenth century, and all non-Muslims were vulnerable to exploitation, extortion, and attack. The situation was particularly unfavorable in Iraq, where the wealthy Jewish community of Baghdad was so oppressed that many (for example, the Sassoon family, ancestors of today's well-known Sassoons) fled to Iran, India, and beyond.

As the nineteenth century wore on, the Jews of the Middle East were becoming more and more Westernized and urbanized, and they were drawn to great cities like Cairo and Alexandria. Traditional patterns of life inherited from the Middle Ages began to break down as all people adopted European dress and patterns of culture and as women began to leave the home to take part in cultural life. From early on in the century, Jews from all over the Middle East had also been going to Palestine, where they were artisans and entrepreneurs; they also began building agricultural settlements and citrus groves there independently of the Zionist settlers from Europe who began arriving late in the century.

As World War I approached, the Jewish communities in the Balkans were disrupted by the local manifestations of nationalism that had troubled the peninsula since the Greek uprising against the Turks in 1821. Each uprising—whether conducted by the Greeks, the Serbs, the Bulgarians, or the Romanians—resulted in the killing of Jews, and this pattern was only intensified during the Balkan wars of 1912–13. When Salonica, one of the great centers

A priest blesses the Montenegran army at the outset of the First Balkan War, 1912–13.

of Sephardic culture, was struck by fire in 1917, the Greek government refused to permit the Jews to resettle their ancient district. Yet during this period, Sephardic culture experienced a late blooming. Jewish newspapers written in French, Turkish, and Ladino appeared in all the major cities of the Balkans and the Ottoman empire, and Ladino fiction and folk poetry flourished.

The Jews of Algeria, who were French citizens, fought vigorously for their country during World War I; but the Tunisian Jews, who were not French citizens, were reluctant, especially in face of the anti-Semitism of French officials in Tunisia. Although not militarily significant, the fact that a Palestinian Jew organized the Zion Mule Corps to fight for the British deserves mention, for this group became the nucleus of the Jewish Legion.

World War I brought an end to the already badly dismembered Ottoman empire and brought much of the Middle East under the control of European powers. The patterns and trends that had affected Jewish life before the war continued along the same lines. Although Morocco, which had become a French protectorate just before the war, became far more hospitable to its Jewish community, conditions deteriorated in Tripoli, Iraq, and Syria.

All these communities were seriously affected by the rise of Arab nationalism. Jews could not very well identify themselves with the Arab nationalist movements because of these groups' Islamic character and exclusionary Arab nature; another impediment was the Jews' traditional status as dhimmis in the Arab world. Westernized and cosmopolitan Egypt was an important exception, for here Jews did join in public life and some affiliated with the nationalist party. But the Jews and Christians of Iraq begged the British occupiers, whom they regarded as their saviors, not to reinstate an Arab government, or at least to grant them British citizenship. During the time that Iraq was a British mandate, Jews and Christians served in the civil service and one Jew even became a cabinet minister; but when Iraq became independent in 1932, Arab nationalist sentiment rejected the employment of non-Muslims in government positions. Meanwhile, Algerian Jews continued to identify with France and set a course of radical assimilation. Thus, in each territory the Jews turned in a different direction for national identity.

In the welter of nationalist movements agitating the Middle East and the Balkans, Zionism (which will be discussed in greater detail in chapter nine) naturally laid claim to the loyalties of many Middle Eastern Jews. Their links with Palestine had always been closer than those of European Jewry, not only because of geographical proximity but also because they had been politically linked during the long Ottoman period. And many Middle Eastern Jews had already emigrated there to engage in commerce and agriculture.

Although Zionist organizations formed first in Egypt, for a long time they attracted mainly Jews of European origin. While Algerian Jews generally rejected Zionism because of their strong identification with France, Tunisian and Moroccan Jewry embraced it energetically. Zionism was at first strong in Syria and Lebanon. But the rise of Arab nationalism, first in Syria, Lebanon, and Iraq, later in other countries, reduced Zionist activity in all these countries and led non-Zionist Jews to try to identify themselves as "Arab Jews." Among the powerful anti-Zionist Jewish forces was the Alliance Israélite Universelle, with its program of assimilation to French culture. By the 1920s, Zionist activity was waning.

The years between 1929 and 1939 saw the deterioration of Jewish-Arab relations throughout the region. This was partly due to the conflict over Palestine, as the growing commitment to a Jewish national homeland headed toward confrontation with growing Arab nationalism. The latter also caused ever greater strains between Middle Eastern populations and the colonial powers, a situation that worked to the disadvantage of both Jews and Christians in the Middle East, since these minorities had identified themselves with the imperialist powers in their desperate efforts to improve their conditions. And with the rise of fascism in Europe, Arab nationalists were provided with a model of extreme nationalism that was particularly attractive because of its association with the enemies of England and

Mustapha Kemal Ataturk (1881–1938), Turkish reformer and first president of the Turkish Republic.

THE LANGUAGES OF THE JEWS: LADINO

The original language of the ancient Israelites was Hebrew, but Hebrew fell out of use as a spoken language by the end of the second century A.D. The Jews generally spoke the prevailing language of whatever place they happened to inhabit. From about 300 B.C. to about A.D. 650, Aramaic and Greek were the main languages of Palestine, and Aramaic was the main language of Iraq. Soon after the arrival of the Arabs in the seventh century, Arabic became the dominant language in the Middle East, and was soon spoken by the Jews of the most important communities, while the Jews of Christian Europe spoke the local vernaculars.

In Spain, Jews spoke the languages of their neighbors: Arabic during the period of Muslim dominance of the peninsula and Spanish when the Christians came to power. The shift was gradual; when it was over, the Jews of Spain were speaking Spanish, singing Spanish folk songs, preparing Spanish foods (modified so as to be kosher), and even reading the Bible in Spanish.

After the explusion of 1492, the Spanish Jews, immensely proud of their cultural heritage, brought their language and customs to their new homes in the eastern Mediterranean. (The Portuguese Jews did the same with their own language, carrying it to Holland and England). Although they often learned the local language, they continued to speak Spanish among themselves. In such places as Turkey and Egypt, their Spanish now appeared to be a Jewish language, for it was spoken by Jews only, not by the local population, which spoke Arabic, Turkish, Greek, and many other languages. Thus, the Spanish of the Jews acquired a Jewish flavor. It came to be called Ladino or Judezmo (that is, Latin or Jewish).

When the Jews spoke Spanish, they mixed in with it some Hebrew words (mostly having to do with Jewish customs and ceremonies) and words from the

local language, mainly Turkish. And since they were cut off from the majority of Spanish speakers in the world, their language did not develop as quickly or in the same ways as the Spanish of Spain or America. The result is that Ladino resembles the Spanish that was spoken in the fifteenth century. It is almost completely intelligible to native Spanish speakers, but it sounds as quaint to them as Elizabethan English would sound to us if we were to encounter a community that still spoke it.

This quaint, old-fashioned quality is a feature not only of the language; it is characteristic of Sephardic culture in general. Thus, Sephardic Jews, to the delight of folklorists, continue to sing the popular songs and ballads of late medieval Spain, and they carry on many customs that have their roots in medieval Iberia.

A page from a 1574 polyglot Bible written in Hebrew with Aramaic, Judeo-Greek, and Ladino translations.

France, the chief occupiers of the Middle East. As the fascist message penetrated the region, it carried with it the Nazi version of European anti-Semitism. Soon *The Protocols of the Elders of Zion*, a seminal European anti-Semitic tract, became widely circulated in Arabic translation throughout the Middle East.

By the end of the 1930s, the position of the Jews had become so reduced that sabotage against Jewish property became routine. Open Zionist activity came to a halt as Jewish community leaders disavowed it in the hope of normalizing relations. The leaders of Egyptian Jewry tried to promote Egypt as a model of peaceful Jewish-Arab cooperation. But there was little the Jews could do to protect themselves against events that were being generated by much larger historical forces.

World War II exacerbated all the negative tendencies. Not only did it convince the Middle Eastern Jews that they had no hope of normal relations with the local population, but it also caused them to be disillusioned with the European powers, to whom they had formerly looked for support. The result was an intense resurgence of Zionism among the region's youth. But despite all this, many Jews continued to hope for a return to normalcy in the postwar period.

It was not to be. The increasing force of Zionism and the increasing force of Arab nationalism continued to move toward confrontation. Anti-Zionist and anti-Jewish riots occured in Egypt, Libya, and Syria. When the United Nations voted to partition Palestine between Jews and Arabs in November 1947, a wave of violence spread throughout the Middle East. Only Morocco was spared.

The end of Jewish life in the Arab world came with the establishment of the State of Israel in 1948. The position of the Jews in most Arab states was now untenable, and they began to stream toward Israel. The Libyan and Yemeni Jewish communities quickly emptied out. The Iraqi Jewish community had nearly entirely emigrated to Israel by 1951. Many Syrian Jews moved to Lebanon, a relatively cosmopolitan and tolerant multiethnic state; many also went to Israel. The situation in Egypt was more complicated—it was mostly the lower classes who went to Israel, while some of the rich moved to Europe or America. But most of the middle and upper classes stayed, and for them, conditions did become somewhat normalized. Large numbers of Jews came to Israel also from Morocco, not so much because of oppression but out of sheer messianic enthusiasm generated by Israel's victory over the Arab League. By the middle of the 1950s, the Jewish communities left in the Arab countries had been reduced to insignificance.

Prime minister David Ben-Gurion reads the Israeli Declaration of Independence in 1948, giving official birth to the State of Israel.

CHAPTER SEVEN

THE JEWS OF EUROPE AND AMERICA

EUROPE

By 1500, when Sephardic Jewry was in flight to the Ottoman empire, Ashkenazic Jewry had for some time been hastening toward resettlement in the East. The Jews were welcomed by the Polish kings because of their high educational level and skills (the Church did not yet have enough influence to counter the kings' economic interest in encouraging Jewish settlement). Whole districts in Poland-Lithuania were settled by Jews, who were permitted to practice crafts, agriculture, and trade. Some Jews also became administrators of nobles' estates or Crown lands, tax farmers, and customs collectors. Thus, the Ashkenazim found a haven of normalcy in eastern Europe parallel to the haven found by the Sephardim in the Ottoman empire.

Like the Sephardim, the Ashkenazim brought their own language with them from their homeland. Though never as integrated into German culture as the Sephardim had been in Spanish culture, the Ashkenazim continued to speak the German language in their new settlements. Their language, already incorporating Hebrew words and expressions, now absorbed Slavic elements and acquired a distinctive character so that it came to be known as Yiddish. Like Ladino, Yiddish is written in the Hebrew alphabet.

OPPOSITE: A street scene on the Lower East Side of New York at the peak of Jewish immigration.

BELOW: The burning of Jews in Deckendorf, Bavaria, in a fifteenth-century woodcut.

Intellectually more insular than the Sephardim, and now freed from the restraints they had long been under, the Ashkenazim threw themselves intensely into religious activity and studies. Talmudic scholarship acquired enormous prestige. Great academies flourished in Lublin, Poznan, and Cracow, and the great trading fairs of Lwow and Lublin became academic recruiting centers where tens of thousands of merchants' sons came to meet with representatives of the schools and to arrange for their studies.

The fairs provided the opportunity for representatives of various communities to meet and make decisions for the governance of the Jews of the territories of eastern Europe. In the sixteenth century, such meetings gave rise to such bodies as the Council of the Four Lands, which controlled the Jewish community of Poland, and the Council of the Land of Lithuania. Though never formally constituted as permanent bodies, they were recognized for practical purposes by the Polish and Lithuanian governments as authoritative. Thus, the Jews achieved some autonomy within the great states of eastern Europe. The councils were abolished in 1764.

Back in central Europe, the Reformation, which began in 1517, seemed to offer the possibility of tolerance with the rise of Protestantism breaking the uniformity of doctrine that had prevailed in the Middle Ages. At the same time, the spread of humanism led to an interest on the part of Christian intellectuals in Jewish writings, especially biblical commentaries and kabbala. In 1513, an odd reversal occurred when a Christian scholar named Reuchlin publically and at personal risk defended the Talmud against the denunciations of a former Jew named Pfefferkorn. Reuchlin's prestige helped to make the study of Hebrew respectable among Christian scholars and influenced the pope to have the first uncensored copy of the Talmud printed.

Early in his career as a religious reformer, Martin Luther seemed to defend the Jews by adding to his attacks on the Catholic Church the accusation that it had been responsible for the unfair persecution of

Portrait of Martin Luther (1483–1546) by Lucas Cranach the Younger (1515–1586).

the Jews. But when Luther saw that the Jews were no more interested in following him than in following the Catholic Church, he turned against them and wrote denunciations so vicious that they seem to anticipate the propaganda of the Nazis four centuries later.

Hardly less harsh was the Catholic reaction to the rise of Protestantism, the Counter Reformation of the mid-sixteenth century. This movement opposed not only Protestants, but the Jews as well, bringing about a resurgence of medieval persecution and repression. These actions struck the Jews of Italy with particular severity, for they had never been subject to the persecutions and massacres that had been typical of the rest of Europe; in fact, the humanist popes of the Renaissance had been friendly toward them in the first part of the sixteenth century.

During the period of the Counter Reformation, the printing of Hebrew books was subjected to censorship. The Counter Reformation also saw the establishment of the first ghettos—walled-in neighborhoods to which Jews were restricted—in Venice

(1516), Rome, Florence, and elsewhere; in other cities, the Jews were simply forced to leave. Thus, Marranos, who had just escaped the Inquisition in Spain to the safe haven of Italy, were now again without protection, and many moved on to the Ottoman empire.

Even in Poland, the tranquillity of Jewish life broke down in the seventeenth century. During Poland's expansion, the Polish nobles had taken control of the Ukraine, where the people, who were Orthodox, resented not only the Poles' conquest of their land but the fact that the foreign overlords were Catholic. Because the Polish nobles left Jewish administrators and tax collectors to manage their new estates and collect taxes, the oppressed Ukranian peasants identified the Jews with the exploitative Polish lords. In 1648, a Cossack leader named Chmielnicki led an uprising of Cossacks and Tatars against the Poles. In the devastation that ensued, Jews throughout the Ukraine were massacred amid atrocities. The revolt spread to Lithuania and White Russia. Sometimes Jews were offered the opportunity to save themselves by converting to Orthodoxy, and the martyrdom that occurred during the First Crusade was repeated. The disorders lasted eight years, and the Jewish population of Poland was significantly reduced. By this point, Jews were emigrating back to western Europe, from where they had come. Although Polish Jewry would eventually recover, its morale was badly scarred. Surely the ardor with which eastern European Jews embraced the messianic claims of Shabbetai Zevi

A nineteenth-century photograph of the Jewish Street in the Lublin Ghetto, Poland.

(see chapter six) was an expression of desperate yearning for an end to their extreme suffering, caused by their anomalous position among nations. All the more devastating was the disappointment that attended news of his failure.

Meanwhile, conditions were improving for the Jews in parts of western Europe. After a long struggle, the Protestant Netherlands had succeeded in freeing itself from the control of Catholic Spain, and in 1579 it proclaimed freedom of religion. Now Marranos from Portugal and, later, from Spain began to stream to Holland and to return to Judaism. At first, there were misunderstandings, for the Dutch suspected the immigrants from Spain, with their mysterious rituals, of being Catholic spies. But when it became clear that the fleeing Marranos feared and hated the Inquisition just as much as the Dutch themselves. they were received with hospitality. As the Iberian autos-da-fé continued to burn Marranos throughout the seventeenth century, the flight of Marranos to the Netherlands continued, and it quickly became home to a major Sephardic Jewish community. Many of the Marranos had been doctors, lawyers, government officials, and churchmen in Spain; as intellectuals, they found a natural home in the Netherlands, which, during its great period of economic expansion, was also a center of humanism. Jews participated actively in this economic expansion, investing in the East and West India Companies.

Jewish life in the Netherlands was not, however, without religious tensions. The returning Marranos, many generations removed from Jewish life, arrived in the Netherlands with little actual experience of Judaism. In their conscientious effort to return to their ancestral religion, they gravitated toward rigid Orthodoxy. Accustomed to living under strict religious control and supervision in Iberia, they now created a community structure that imposed an unnaturally rigid standard of religious belief and observance on its members. This rigidity contrasted with the humanistic atmosphere of religious toleration that prevailed in the Netherlands in general and

therefore repelled many gifted persons. A particularly poignant case was that of Uriel da Costa, who, as a young Catholic clergyman in Portugal, had a desire to return to the dimly remembered religion of his ancestors. He fled to Amsterdam in 1618 and joined the Jewish community there. But his religious doubts persisted, and he was excommunicated. On his second attempt to be reconciled with the Jewish community, the ceremony of penance that was imposed upon him was so humiliating that he committed suicide after undergoing it.

The case of Benedict Spinoza was historically more significant because of Spinoza's great stature. Born in Amsterdam in 1632, Spinoza received a thorough rabbinic education and went on to study philosophy—first the great medieval Jewish philosophers like Maimonides, then such modern philosophers as Descartes. These studies led him to place reason ahead of divine revelation and tradition as a source of knowledge and therefore to reject Judaism as a religious system. The rigid Amsterdam Jewish

Benedict Spinoza, whose rationalism earned him the epithet *L'Athée Juif*—"The Atheist Jew."

LEGENDS OF THE JEWS IN POLAND

The first reliable information about Jews in Poland dates from 1098, when persecution caused the Jews to migrate eastward, though Ashkenazic Jews had been coming to Poland as peddlers and traders as early as the tenth century. In fact, little is known about Poland generally in this early period. Both Jews and Poles attempted to fill the gap with legends. The Poles told of legendary princes named Popiel and Piast who supposedly lived in the ninth century. According to the Jewish version of this legend, when Popiel died in the town of Kruszwica, it proved impossible to reach an agreement on his successor. It was therefore decided that whoever should enter the town first on the following day would be chosen. That person turned out to be a Jew named Abraham Prochownik. (The name alone indicates that this is a legend, for Prochownik means "dusty," or "dust-covered," an apt epithet for a traveling peddler. In later versions of the story, the name was understood to mean "gunpowder," indicating that Abraham was a gunpowder dealer; but gunpowder had not yet been introduced to Europe at that early date.) When Abraham tried to refuse the crown, he was given three days to come to a decision and told that if he still refused, he would be killed. At the end of the period, a group of Poles led by Piast approached his lodgings to crown him. Abraham thereupon pointed to Piast himself, arguing that he was a more suitable candidate, and this suggestion was adopted; Piast became the first Polish king, and was the founder of a legendary dynasty.

According to another legend, the Jews of Germany at the end of the ninth century appealed to Prince Leszek to admit them to Poland because of the pressure they were under in the Holy Roman Empire. Polish place names like Zhydowo, Zhydatycze, and Zhydowska Wola were said to have originated as Jewish villages (*Zhyd* is Polish for "Jew"); historians have proved this claim false.

Much later, during the period of Jewish prosperity in Poland before the Chmielnicki uprising (discussed in this chapter), there was a wealthy Jewish merchant named Saul Wahl (he was a real historical personage who lived from 1541 to c. 1617) who is said by legend to have exercised some royal functions during the interregnum in 1587. According to one version of the legend, he was actually king of Poland for a single day before the ratification of the election of Sigismund III.

According to Jewish legend, the very name of Poland is Hebrew. In the thirteenth century, Jews fleeing the violent persecutions in central Europe reached the forests of Poland. Finding the peasants friendly, and anti-Semitism still unknown, they are supposed to have said, in Hebrew, "Po lin," meaning "Tarry here," giving the land its name.

The Jewish quarter Kazimlesz in Cracow, around 1800.

community could not tolerate such nonconformity and excommunicated him. After his excommunication, he wrote a series of works on religion and ethics that eventually won him acclaim as a philosopher, but the Dutch Jewish community, still medieval in its outlook, was not ready to harbor, much less to venerate, a major modern thinker like Spinoza. He died in 1677.

Another window of toleration for Jews was Hamburg. Toward the end of the sixteenth century, a small colony of Portuguese Marranos arrived to participate in the commercial prosperity of this tiny but thriving state. The newcomers had great wealth and international commercial connections and were made welcome as long as they were thought to be "ordinary" Portuguese. When it became known that they were actually Portuguese Jews, though, efforts were made, mainly by the clergy, to dislodge them. But their resources were needed, and when the Jews threatened to move to Denmark, the Hamburg senate extended their privileges.

England finally began to reverse the expulsion of 1290 during the mid-seventeenth century. The doors did not open suddenly or even officially, but by the latter part of the century Jews could again live openly in England. Individual Spanish and Portuguese Marranos had begun to trickle in during the reign of Elizabeth I, and she herself had a Marrano physician—though he was executed on suspicion of trying to poison her. During the reign of Charles I (1625–49), Marranos rose in wealth and power, but when it came to light that they were Jews, the problem of whether they could be tolerated arose. The Puritan revolution of 1649 favored the admission of the Jews because of Puritan admiration of the Old Testament, and Cromwell personally believed that Jewish merchants could make a positive contribution to English commerce. In 1655, a famous rabbi of Amsterdam, Menasseh ben Israel (1604–57), sailed to England to present Cromwell with his petition that the Jews be readmitted to England and that they be allowed to practice their religion openly. Because of pressure from the clergy and because of local merchants' fear of competition from the newcomers, though, the proposal was not adopted. But Cromwell gave the Marranos oral permission to remain in England and treated Menasseh ben Israel with honors. In 1656, the Marranos in London were granted permission to assemble for prayers and to establish a cemetery. In 1664, Charles II assured the community of continued toleration.

Meanwhile, in central Europe, conditions were slowly developing that allowed individual Jews to amass great wealth and power. The many tiny German states formed after the Thirty Years' War (1618–48) were constantly in need of funds, and the Jews remaining in these territories were experts in

A Jewish woman on her way to the synagogue.

finance, thanks to centuries of legislation that had made moneylending their people's chief means of gaining a livelihood. Hence, Jews were brought into the petty German-speaking courts as financiers and financial advisers. Their duties were gradually extended into other areas until a whole class of court Jews emerged. Exempted from many of the restrictions borne by the majority of Jews, these people received titles and honors, and sometimes even socialized with their masters.

Thus, Samuel Oppenheimer of Vienna was able to obtain the credits that allowed the Austrians to fight the French in the 1670s and the Turks in the 1680s, when the Turkish army stood before the very walls of Vienna. But in 1700, a mob stormed his house and destroyed his books, and he died bankrupt because of the failure of the Austrian treasury to pay its debts to him. Indeed, the position of the court Jews was precarious, for the most part, and they were often hated by the Christian masses. And despite whatever privileges the court Jews did enjoy, the masses of Jews living in the German territories continued to live under medieval restrictions, unmitigated by the pretensions of the age to be the Age of Enlightenment.

But the eighteenth century saw intellectual changes that would make possible the emergence of the Jews into modernity. A new concept of statehood emerged, which was based on a direct relationship between the individual and the state rather than on a network of autonomous and semiautonomous bodies (such as the Jewish community). One law was now to apply to all citizens. These changes exposed the Jews to opportunities that had formerly been denied them, allowing them access to a greater variety of livelihoods and thereby improving their economic condition; but they also made it harder for the Jews to maintain their communal cohesiveness. Now it became possible for individual Jews to advance their own positions at the cost of abandoning their Jewish identity for that of another nationality, such as French or German. This problem has remained with the Jews down to our own time.

Menasseh ben Israel in 1642.

Many intellectuals assumed that the Jews would simply be absorbed into the body of the state. This approach was legislated by Austrian emperor Joseph II in 1782, who granted the Jews in his realm some tax relief while instituting measures for encouraging their social and linguistic assimilation. His intention was to "improve" the Jews, make them more useful for society, and prepare them gradually for full civil rights if they should come to deserve them. A more sympathetic approach was taken by the political philosopher John Toland in England, who argued in

1714 that simply granting the Jews civil rights would make them more useful and productive.

One of the chief proponents of a sympathetic approach to the Jews was the German thinker Gotthold Ephraim Lessing, who argued for the equal treatment of the Jews as human beings, despite religious and social differences. In this, he was influenced by the Jewish philosopher Moses Mendelssohn (1729–86), who reformulated the basic ideas of Judaism in the spirit of the Enlightenment, enabling him to argue that the Jewish tradition was not a debased religion but was actually a model of the highest ideals of the age. Although completely loyal to the Jewish tradition, Mendelssohn was also completely at home in the world of Enlightenment philosophy, and he impressed many influential non-Jewish thinkers through his writings and his personality.

The French Revolution, after initial hesitation, offered full civil rights to those Jews who were willing to be assimilated into French culture; it refused to deal with the Jews as members of a separate entity. When Napoleon came to power, he modified this position, maintaining the tradition of equality for the Jews, but reviving the medieval idea of creating a leadership body to represent them and to execute his plans regarding them. The result was the creation in 1806 of the Assembly of Jewish Notables and the French Sanhedrin to give religious sanction to the Assembly's resolutions. (This Sanhedrin declared it a religious duty of Jews to regard the state in which they were born or had settled as their fatherland.) In practice, though, Napoleon limited the legal equality of the Jews. Even so, the legal position of the Jews continued to improve in France throughout the nineteenth century.

After the fall of the Napoleonic empire, the Congress of Vienna refused to ratify the rights of the Jews acquired under the empire, and in 1819 violent anti-Semitic riots called the "Hep! Hep!" disturbances sprang up in Germany. Throughout the rest of the century, the various German states would grant civil rights to Jews, retract them, and reenact

TOP: Gotthold Ephraim Lessing (1729–1781)

BOTTOM: Moses Mendelssohn (1729–1786)

The attack on the Palais Royal during the French Revolution.

them. In England, the process was smoother, culminating when a professing Jew became a member of Parliament in 1858.

Despite the halting process by which the Jews of western Europe became emancipated, many were able to achieve considerable personal success. The Rothschilds of Frankfurt, the Pereiras of France, and the Bleichroeders of Prussia built banking empires, and Baron de Hirsch, a Jewish estate owner in Bavaria, financed railroad construction. But even on a less spectacular scale, many Jews did well under the improved circumstances. They were especially attracted to medicine, law, journalism, and literature; they also populated the lower ranks of academia (university chairs were generally not available to them).

But during this process, Jews converted to Christianity by the thousands, partly in order to smooth their paths to the opportunities now within their reach, partly because the old ways simply had come to seem old-fashioned, and partly because

The five Rothschild brothers, sons of Mayer Amschel Rothschild (1744–1812), who established branches of the Rothschild banking firm in most of the major commercial centers of Europe.

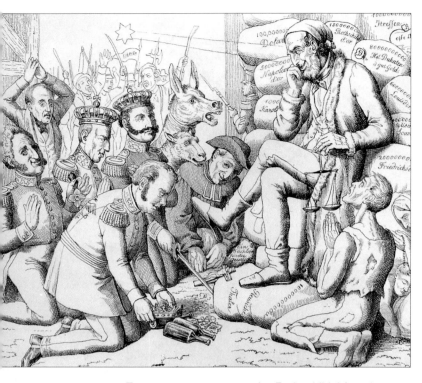

ABOVE: European potentates at the Rothschilds' feet, in an anti-Semitic cartoon from nineteenth-century Frankfurt.

BELOW: This watercolor, c. 1810, from a series of "Vienna Types," shows three Jews in front of a state lottery office and a tobacco shop. The Jews have coarse features typical of anti-Semitic depictions.

many, genuinely attracted by the universalist outlook of the Enlightenment, could no longer adhere to a religion that seemed to reject the high culture of the age. Enlightened religious leaders attempted to counter this destructive tendency through religious reform, using liberal German Protestantism as the model. They attempted to redefine Judaism as a pure religious and moral system, rejecting the principle of Jewish ethnic and national identity along with many of the rituals that were associated with that identity and that tended to mark the Jews as alien. One of the great representatives of this trend was Abraham Geiger (1810–74). More radical reformers wished to abolish all religious impediments to integration with non-Jews, such as the dietary laws and the prohibition on mixed marriages; they also wished to abolish the hope for the restoration of the Davidic kingdom, a major theme of the liturgy, and the use of Hebrew in prayer. More moderate reformers, such as Zacharias Frankel (1801–75), demanded an approach that would remain truer to the historical experience of the Jewish people.

The first major institutional step toward religious reform was the founding of the Hamburg temple in 1818, and the issuing of its reformed prayer book, which was based on the Portuguese rite and included prayers in German instead of Hebrew. Such changes were controversial and occasioned considerable upheaval within the German and Austrian Jewish communities. The outcome was the side-by-side existence of Orthodox and Reform congregations in these countries, and, after 1840, in London.

Given the centrifugal forces of the time, Jewish communal organizations lost much of their hold. In central Europe, as religious reform took hold of the leadership of the Jewish community, the community structures fragmented, as the Orthodox split off and created their own organizations. But in some places, communal organizations were strengthened. Napoleon instituted the consistory system under which Jewish affairs were administered by regional committees, or consistories, of rabbis and laymen, communal bodies that could be used to impose state policies. In England, the Board of Deputies was established, which, under the chairmanship of the great philanthropist Moses Montefiore, acted on behalf of the Jews of the entire British empire; in the second half of the nineteenth century, the office of chief rabbi was established.

The situation of the Jews in eastern Europe was quite different. The vast Jewish population of Poland was dismembered when Poland was partitioned toward the end of the eighteenth century among Austria, Prussia, and Russia, and the bulk of the Jewish population fell to Russia. In 1804, Czar Alexander I issued measures designed to "improve" the Jews in order to prepare them for civil rights. One such measure was to expel them from the towns, thereby separating them from the peasants. Another measure created the Pale of Jewish Settlement, which defined the area in which Jews were permitted to live. This area included the regions acquired from Poland plus several districts in the southeastern part of the state. The rule was to remain in effect until the Russian Revolution. Thus, the Jews were driven to a limited territory, and within that territory they were driven away from the villages to the cities.

The expulsions from the villages in the Pale resulted in the growth of the Jewish market towns. Supported by shopkeepers, craftsmen, and peddlers, the economy of each of these towns, called *shtetls* in Yiddish, was centered on a marketplace. The shtetls became home to the vast majority of the Jewish population. Only a handful of Jews were able to enter Russia and enrich themselves in large-scale business, and a Jewish city proletariat emerged only slowly.

In 1827, the Russian government established a quota of Jewish youths to be supplied for prolonged army service—usually twenty-five years. The intention was to use the army as a means for weaning the soldiers (known as Cantonists) away from their Jewish heritage and assimilating them into Russian life. This edict caused considerable tension within the Jewish community, as the community leaders were suspected by the poor of evading it, while using the poor's children to fill the quota. Further measures designed to encourage assimilation were enacted by successive czars, the tendency being generally to reward the more assimilated Jews and penalize those who were less assimilated.

Abraham Geiger (1810–1874), militant early leader of the Reform movement in Judaism and an outstanding academic scholar of Judaism.

The vast majority of eastern European Jews continued to live traditional lives, unaffected by the religious reform that was so distinctively a feature of western European Jewry. But they were not uniform in religious style, nor were they unaffected by the intellectual trends of the age. The eighteenth century had seen the rise of a popular pietistic-mystical movement known as Hasidism, founded by Israel Baal Shem (c. 1700–60). This movement, which stressed ecstatic worship, catered to the masses rather than to the learned elite. It was organized around the leadership of charismatic rabbis, called *zaddikim*, who established in dozens of shtetls courts that became the object of pilgrimage by their adherents. The movement thrived despite bitter attacks by the great Lithuanian scholar-rabbis, especially Elijah of Vilna (1720–97). Perceiving Hasidism as a threat, the Lithuanian rabbis created anti-Hasidic schools and patterns of religious behavior. Thus emerged the two orthodox movements of eastern Europe, that of the Hasidim and that of their opponents, the *mitnagedim*. Both movements survived the decimation of Jewish life in Europe and both have experienced a resurgence in our own time, far from their original homelands and from the conditions under which they originally arose.

The 1866 opening of the new synagogue in Berlin.

PERSONALITIES: LEONE DE MODENA

Born in Venice in 1571, where he spent most of his life, Modena is an outstanding representative of Italian Renaissance Jewry. In Ferrara, where he was raised, he was considered a child prodigy, for at the age of two and a half he read the portion from the prophets in the synagogue service, and at three he could translate parts of the Torah from Hebrew into Italian. He mastered not only rabbinic studies, but also Italian and Latin. He became famous in his youth for his linguistic acrobatics, translating Italian poetry into Hebrew verse and composing (at age thirteen!) a poem that made sense whether it was read as Hebrew or Italian.

Modena did not pursue any single profession, but supported himself by various intellectual pursuits. His mainstay was preaching. Although sermons had always been an important part of the synagogue service, they were not developed into an art form until the Renaissance. Modena's sermons, delivered in Italian in accordance with the rhetorical style of contemporary public speaking, were considered exemplary, and his appearances became public events. In an age of expanded intellectual curiosity, even non-Jewish scholars would crowd the synagogue to attend Modena's brilliant performances.

Modena also wrote Hebrew verse as a means of support, particularly verses to be used as tombstone inscriptions in the cemetery of Venice. He translated documents and ghostwrote letters, poems, and sermons for others. He even wrote a comedy and acted in amateur theatrical performances. Modena had some musical ability, holding a position in the Jewish musical academy in the ghetto of Venice; he championed the introduction of the liturgical music of the Jewish composer Salomone de Rossi into the synagogue service. He experimented with alchemy, resulting in the death of his beloved son by lead poisoning. Altogether, Modena lists twenty-six occupations that he pursued during his colorful life. One of his most precious writings was his autobiography, written in Hebrew, a poignant document of the unhappy life of a gifted but unstable person.

One of the causes of Modena's unhappiness was his poverty, which he recognized was in large measure due to his compulsive gambling. Time and again he vowed to avoid bad company, save his earnings, and put his life on an even keel; but he never succeeded. His unsettled nature was passed on to two of his sons, who led disreputable lives. The frankness of Modena's autobiography makes it a very modern-sounding document.

But Modena's weaknesses did not prevent him from being taken seriously by influential people. One of his important works, *Historia de' riti Ebraici* (*History of the Jewish Rites*), was written on commission for King James I of England. Most of Modena's voluminous writings, which address most of the important Jewish intellectual issues of the age, are in Hebrew.

Leone de Modena, one of the foremost Jewish thinkers of the Renaissance.

ABOVE: Sir Moses Montefiore (1784–1885).

BELOW: Residents of the Durashna shtetl, photographed in 1929.

THE UNITED STATES

Toward the end of the nineteenth century, a major population shift occurred, one that marked the beginning of the gradual decline of eastern Europe as the major center of European Jewish life. This was the large-scale movement of Jews from Slavic lands to the United States.

The mass emigration of the Jews from eastern Europe was precipitated by some specific events, such as the pogroms of 1881–83 and the upheavals in Russia between 1903 and 1907. But the main reason was poverty. The Jewish population of eastern Europe had grown to 6.8 million in the course of the nineteenth century, but Russian restrictions excluded Jews from the new industrial cities as well as from agriculture, forcing them into hopeless misery. Emigration was the only solution; America was the obvious goal.

The first Jewish settlers in North America were a group of twenty-three Jewish refugees from Brazil who settled in New Amsterdam in 1654, but they did not establish a permanent community there. After the arrival of the British, Sephardic Jews began to arrive, later to be joined by Ashkenazim, who, however, tended to adopt Sephardic customs. Most of the Jewish settlers supported the American Revolution, and one Jewish merchant, Haym Salomon, was instrumental in raising funds for the war's final campaigns. After independence, Jewish traders began to move into the South and other Jews went into finance and the professions. As immigration from Europe continued, the Jewish community came to be dominated by Ashkenazim, but it remained tiny until about 1840.

The number of Jews in America was greatly augmented in the middle of the nineteenth century by large-scale immigration of German-speaking Jews from Germany, Bohemia, and Hungary. German-Jewish peddlers traveled and settled throughout the country, even as far away as California, where they supplied the gold prospectors. Although recognition

ABOVE: Elijah of Vilna, known as the Vilna Gaon (1720–97), Talmudic scholar and opponent of Hasidism.

BELOW: Living conditions in Poland during World War I.

of the Jews' rights to be treated as full citizens did not occur automatically with the adoption of the Constitution in 1788 (the Constitution regulated only federal, not state, law), anti-Semitism was negligible during this period.

The immigration of central European Jews brought with it both a large number of Jews who were more learned in the tradition than the earlier arrivals and a large number of Jews who had the experience of Reform Judaism. The first Reform congregation in the United States was founded in Charleston, South Carolina, in 1824, and the movement took root with the founding of the Emanu-El Reformverein in New York. The tendency was toward a liberal and rational version of Judaism that would harmonize with life in the New World and enable the Jews to live like full American citizens. In Albany, and later in Cincinnati, Rabbi Isaac Mayer Wise became a major figure in the development of the institutions of American Reform Judaism.

Immigration from central Europe continued after the American Civil War. German Jews and Reform Judaism clearly dominated American Jewry, so that

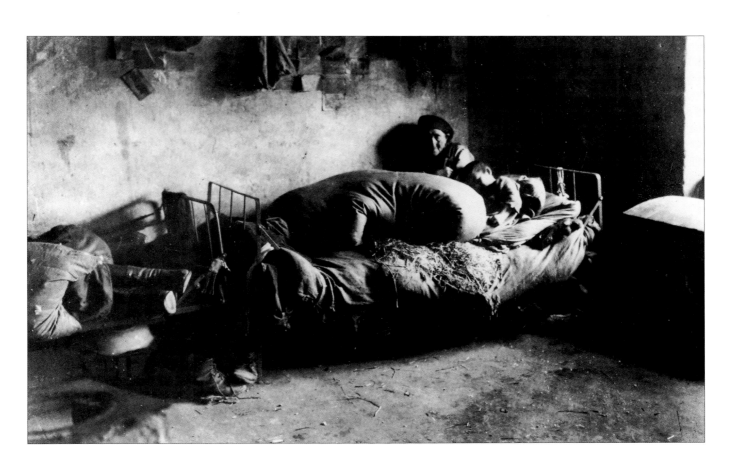

by 1880, when Jews in the United States numbered some 280,000, Reform Judaism was synonymous with American Judaism. The movement's principles were defined in the Pittsburgh Platform of 1885, and its main institutions, the Union of American Hebrew Congregations and the Hebrew Union College, were founded in 1873 and 1875 respectively.

But the character of American Jewry was radically and permanently altered by the vast migratory movement from eastern Europe that began in 1880. When it was over, around 1929, the numbers had risen to 4.5 million. By 1918, the Jewish community of the United States was the largest in the world.

The immediate effect was the creation of huge Jewish districts in all the major cities, especially in older slum areas. Some immigrants became small retailers, but the vast majority became workers, especially in the garment industry, which quickly became a distinctively Jewish field. The brutal working conditions in the sweatshops where clothing was manufactured sparked Jewish involvement in the labor movement. With the growing industrialization of

TOP LEFT: Victims of a pogrom in Proskurov, Ukraine, in February 1919, with mourners.

TOP RIGHT: Children wounded in a pogrom near Kiev.

ABOVE: Jewish self-defense force in Chernobyl in 1919.

ABOVE: Jatkowa (Meatmarket) Street in the old Jewish quarter of Vilna.

BELOW: Polish and Russian Social Democrats and members of the Bund honoring victims of the Vilna pogrom of 1905. The Bund was a Jewish socialist party founded in Russia in 1897.

clothing manufacturing after the turn of the century and with the arrival of experienced labor organizers after the collapse of the Russian revolutionary movement in 1906, unionism gained strength.

The concentration of the Jewish population in the big cities permitted a burst of cultural activity conducted in Yiddish. Yiddish newspapers appeared, as well as theater, radio programs, and lectures; there were even Yiddish music publishers. Primarily secular in content, Yiddish cultural activity was, however, nostalgic for the folkways of the old country. It was fostered by the Jewish labor movement, especially the Workmen's Circle, which also provided social benefits. Help was provided for Jewish immigrants by hometown associations, called *landsmanshaftn*, as well. And during this time, hundreds of tiny synagogues sprang up to serve the immigrants.

Haym Salomon, whose fundraising was crucial to the success of the American Revolution.

The established German-Jewish population of the United States took a mixed attitude toward the Eastern European newcomers. On the one hand, the longer-settled German Jews regarded the Yiddish-speaking immigrants as uncouth and embarrassing because of their poverty and cultural backwardness, which they feared would be prejudicial to their own hard-won acceptance in American society. On the other hand, the German Jews also felt a responsibility to help the new immigrants overcome the hardships of their immigrant status. The two attitudes were not wholly unrelated, for many established Jews felt that the only way to escape the embarrassment of the unrefined eastern Europeans was to provide them with the means to become settled and Americanized. Various charities and educational institutions were established to this end.

Some of the established Jews worried that the process of acculturation was too rapid and that it was leading the younger generation to reject their ancestral religion in exchange for radical social doctrines or mere hedonism. New York's Jewish Theological Seminary of America, founded in 1887, was reorganized in 1902 under the leadership of Solomon Schechter to provide for the training of modern English-speaking rabbis who could appeal to the first native generation. Schechter was a distinguished academic scholar of Judaism, having taught rabbinic literature at Cambridge. As a religious leader, he strove to build institutions to propagate the kind of liberalized but historically correct Judaism that had been promoted in Germany by Zecharias Frankel. Thus, Conservative Judaism came into being as a third religious movement, existing alongside Reform Judaism and the variety of Orthodox institutions established by the immigrants. As a middle-of-the-road movement, its natural appeal to second-generation Jews made it the largest of the three movements in America for much of the twentieth century.

The turn toward isolationism after World War I and the "Red Scare" of 1919–20 aroused strong negative feelings against foreigners and considerable fervor for Americanization. These attitudes were

TOP LEFT: Freight trains carrying Jewish emigrants to Gdansk.

TOP RIGHT: A demonstration against the pogroms in London, July 7, 1919.

ABOVE: Samuel Hirszenberg's representation of the pogroms: *The Black Banner* (1905).

BELOW LEFT: Jews bewailing the loss of their home in Sochoczow, Poland.

BELOW RIGHT: Corpses of Jews killed during the pogrom of October 22, 1905, in Odessa.

TOP: The Red Star-American Line shipping office in Warsaw during the period of Jewish emigration.

ABOVE: In Warsaw, waiting to embark for the free city of Gdansk (Danzig).

directed particularly against Jews because so many of them were prominent among political radicals. Jews had to hear themselves attacked by such men as Henry Ford as being racially inferior members of an international plot to overthrow Western civilization. And the Ku Klux Klan, which gained wide political power during the early 1920s, added Jews to blacks and Catholics as its targets. In the long run, the most significant effect of these tendencies was the Johnson Act of 1924, which gradually restricted immigration.

During the prosperity of the 1920s, large numbers of Jews entered the professions and white-collar occupations, despite restrictions against their employment in large life-insurance firms, banks, law firms, and retail chains. The road to the professions was made difficult for many by quotas in universities, especially medical schools. Nevertheless, the children of the immigrants gravitated toward these fields, and the representation of Jews in labor gradually diminished. Jews were also attracted to intellectual work, and they soon became prominent in publishing and entertainment, especially in motion pictures.

The Depression, which began in 1929, put a severe strain on Jewish charitable organizations and increased discrimination against Jews in employment. But Jews continued to be attracted to business and the professions, benefitting particularly from the fact that a high-quality free college education was available in such cities as New York. Continuing anti-Semitic propaganda during this time was particularly disturbing to American Jews against the background of the rise of Nazism in Germany; President Franklin Roosevelt was seen as a hero because of his vehement opposition to Nazism and his rejection of anti-Semitism.

The anti-Jewish legislation in Germany of the 1930s created another small wave of Jewish immigration, driving some 33,000 German Jews to the United States. Many of these people had to adjust to a difficult life, given the unfavorable economic conditions of the depression era. Among them were thousands of intellectuals and scientists (including Albert Einstein), who were soon wielding great influence on many areas of American intellectual life. Thus, Hitler's actions were responsible for the wholesale transfer of Jewish intellectual leadership from Europe to the United States during this decade.

By this time, millions of European Jews had made America their home. Despite hardships, they had improved their situation dramatically and could look forward optimistically to the future. Still, millions of Jews remained behind in central and eastern Europe. On the eve of World War II, the Jewish population of the United States was about half that of Europe. Only six years later, the Jewish population of Europe would be almost completely wiped out.

TOP: Immigrants, having passed through the receiving station at Ellis Island, at Battery Park in New York City.

ABOVE: Storefronts on the Lower East Side of New York around 1930. The sign in Yiddish announces the opening of a new grocery on the site.

CHAPTER EIGHT

THE DESTRUCTION OF EUROPEAN JEWRY

Among the expulsions, pogroms, and simple humiliations experienced by the Jews over the course of the centuries, the destruction of European Jewry during the period from 1933 to 1945 belongs to a select list of disasters that includes the destruction of the Second Temple, the First Crusade, and the expulsion from Spain.

The Jews of Germany had won civil rights in the course of the nineteenth century, and the great majority of them had made use of this opportunity to accept enthusiastically not only German citizenship, but also German culture and identity. We have seen how the Germanization of the Jews of central Europe weakened their links to the Jewish tradition, often leading to intermarriage and complete assimilation. But the medieval legacy could not be so quickly suppressed—a legacy of centuries in which the Jews were a mysterious, alien population in the midst of Europe, and in which the Church taught that the Jews deserved to be kept in humiliation because of their obduracy in not accepting Christianity. The pressures of the postwar period brought the deeply rooted antipathy of Germans toward the Jews to the surface.

Humiliated by their defeat in World War I and the extreme measures imposed on them by the victorious allies and suffering from economic crisis, many Germans turned hostile to the outside world and embraced extreme nationalism. Among the leaders of extremist political organizations, Adolf Hitler succeeded in creating a lasting movement, the National

Socialist (or Nazi) party, and bringing it to power in January 1933. There was no revolution or armed takeover of the German government. The Nazis came to power through the legal manipulation of the democratic system under which Germany was governed during the postwar period, the so-called Weimar Republic, with its advanced constitution and liberal principles. Nazi control of the government was duly confirmed by elections held on March 5, 1933, at which 44 percent of the electorate voted in favor of the Nazi party.

OPPOSITE: The synagogue in Baden-Baden burning on the Night of Broken Glass.

ABOVE: German-Jewish soldiers observing the Day of Atonement of 1890 in an army camp in Metz.

The Nazis had from the very beginning taken the position that the German and Nordic people generally belonged to a distinct and superior race of humans known as the Aryans, a race distinguished by beauty, vigor, and intelligence. Below the Aryans were the inferior races: the Mediterranean peoples, the Slavic peoples, and, at the bottom, the Jews, who were, according to the Nazis, a genetically criminal race devoted to corrupting and undermining civilization. The Jews were thought to be especially guilty because of their behavior in Germany: they had supposedly insinuated themselves into German society, intermarrying in order to impair its genetic superiority, serving in its armed forces in order to betray it, and entering its universities so as to undermine its intellectual life; Jewish businessmen supposedly competed unfairly with German firms, enriching themselves, impoverishing ordinary German workers, and engineering the

economic crisis; and the defeat of Germany in World War I had been the result of Jewish treachery. The motto was, "The Jews are our misfortune." In his book *Mein Kampf* (1925–27), Hitler had dwelled on the necessity of exterminating the Jewish race in order to secure the recovery of Germany. This attitude was a major part of the platform of the Nazi party, whose power, it is important to remember, was confirmed by popular vote.

The policy of the Nazi party was to make Germany free of Jews, forcing them to emigrate by making their lives unbearable. As early as April 1, 1933, a carefully organized nationwide boycott of Jewish businesses and professional offices was held. The following week, the term "non-Aryan" was adopted as a legal designation to facilitate separating the Jews out of society. One by one, professions were closed to persons so designated. In 1935, the Nuremberg Laws

Hitler and other Nazi leaders reviewing the German troops in 1933.

Young German fascists at a mass march in Berlin, their arms raised in the famous Nazi salute.

were adopted, depriving Jews of citizenship, prohibiting intermarriage, and imposing other restrictions, which were amplified from time to time.

Random violence, arrests, and humiliations directed at the Jewish population by government officials and members of the Nazi militias soon followed. In 1933, signs reading "Jews not wanted" were posted in businesses, cafés, and sports stadiums, and on roadsides all over the country; Jewish names were scratched out of war memorials; and posters threatening violence against Jews were to be seen everywhere. Before long, even park benches had signs on them restricting their use by Jews.

The Jews were slow to realize that the anti-Semitic policies of the government would not be reversed and that emigration was their only option. Most of them truly believed that they were Germans and that their fellow citizens would eventually come to their senses and force the government to reverse its poli-

cies. Had Jewish patriots not fought alongside non-Jewish patriots in the World War? But the Jews discovered, to their horror and disbelief, that most of their friends and neighbors either approved the government's policies toward them, were indifferent to their plight, or were unwilling to take the risk of fighting government policy.

Moreover, thousands of the German Jews were only dimly aware of their families' Jewish past. Many were descended from converts to Christianity or were themselves converts or children of mixed marriages. For these and many others, Jewish identity was merely an unpleasant memory that played little part in their actual lives; they could hardly grasp that to other Germans—sometimes their own relations—they had suddenly become pariahs.

When Germany annexed Austria in March 1938, even more extreme measures were imposed, with even broader popular support. The same occurred

Thousands of German troops listen as Hitler speaks at the Nuremberg Rally of 1936. Such rallies were carefully staged to instill in the German nation a feeling of overwhelming might.

when the Germans invaded the Sudetenland later in 1938. But the worst incident was the one known as *Kristallnacht* (The Night of Broken Glass), which occurred on the night of November 9–10. During Kristallnacht, Jewish property was attacked throughout Germany and Austria. The German government, which had engineered the attacks, claimed that they were a spontaneous popular reprisal for the killing of a German official by a Jew. The Jews were fined one billion marks, and new regulations were imposed to advance the Aryanization of economic life. Mass arrests resulted in the internment of vast numbers in concentration camps; children were expelled from the schools; and Jewish cultural and economic life was brought to a stop.

Now emigration began in earnest as most Jews, even those with big businesses and extensive properties, realized that they had no choice but to flee. To facilitate this process, the government set up an agency in Vienna that accelerated emigration and appropriated Jewish property. The government's intention was not only to free Germany of Jews but also to provoke anti-Semitic reactions in the countries that would be overwhelmed by Jewish immigration. This policy was continued until late 1941, when emigration was prohibited.

By 1939, Hitler's thinking and public pronouncements shifted from merely forcing the Jews out of Germany toward murdering them outright.

After Germany invaded Poland, on September 1, 1939, the anti-Jewish regulations were applied to the occupied territories as they fell to the German military machine. The destruction of Jewry in these territories was given priority even over military interests. Manpower and transport needed by the armed forces were diverted to the war against the Jews and

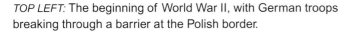

TOP LEFT: The beginning of World War II, with German troops breaking through a barrier at the Polish border.

TOP RIGHT: "Get out, pig!" Anti-Jewish slogan and caricature daubed on the display window of a Jewish shop during the Night of Broken Glass.

ABOVE: A successful German-Jewish business: a manufacturer and retailer of linens in Berlin before World War I.

ABOVE RIGHT: A crowd gathered to stare at the damage to a Jewish stationery shop in Magdeburg on the morning after the Night of Broken Glass (November 9–10, 1938).

RIGHT: Jewish refugees on the French ship *Flandres* as the ship docks in St. Nazaire, France, on June 19, 1939. The ninety-seven German and Czech Jews aboard had been refused admisson to Mexico and were returned to Europe.

CONCENTRATION CAMPS

The first German concentration camps were not specifically designed for Jews; their purpose was to isolate all persons suspected of opposition to the Nazi regime. Among the earliest camps was Dachau, established in 1933, just outside Munich. The early detainees were communists, trade-union members, and socialists, as well as Jewish writers, journalists, and lawyers. Later, these groups were joined by Jehovah's Witnesses and homosexuals. When the camps were first established, the judiciary demanded a warrant for each arrest, though the detention was for an unlimited period. But in 1936, the Gestapo (secret police) were authorized to detain anyone they chose without court supervision, and the concentration camps themselves were put under Gestapo control. At this time, Dachau was enlarged, and new camps were established at Sachsenhausen and Buchen-

wald. In 1937, Jews began to be interned solely on account of being Jewish (rather than as members of other proscribed groups).

Crowding in the camps became a problem after the annexation of Austria and the Night of Broken Glass in 1938 (see page 116). In the following year, Jews began being interned for violations of petty discriminatory rules (like sitting on park benches), as well as for violating the racial purity laws. But until World War II, Jews could gain release from the camps if they could prove that they were able to leave Germany. In fact, during 1939, the number of Jewish internees actually dropped.

With the onset of World War II, the nature of the camps changed; they were no longer intended merely for sequestration but for the exploitation of the prisoners' labor and for extermination. Under the pretext of

Jews in the Warsaw ghetto being rounded up for transport. This is one of the most famous photographs of World War II.

security, the number of internments was vastly increased. Many new camps were built, including Auschwitz and Majdanek (both in Poland). By 1942, the number of internees had grown from 25,000 before the war to 100,000. By 1944, their number had reached one million.

Even before the formalization of the plan for the mass extermination of the Jews, the camps had been used for group exterminations, as in the euthanasia program for killing the mentally and chronically ill; or the program in Ravensbrück (an all-women's camp) for gassing pregnant Jewish women. Beginning in 1941, several camps were provided with crematoria for disposing of the bodies not chosen for medical study in the universities; the prisoners who worked in the crematoria were regularly executed so that information would not escape the camps.

Also in 1941, camps specifically designed as extermination camps were established, in order to mechanize the work being done by the mobile killing units that followed the German troops into the Soviet Union (see page 120). At first, carbon monoxide from trucks was used, but this system was replaced in 1942 with a system of gas chambers disguised as showers. The system reached peak efficiency when an insecticide called Zyklon-B (manufactured by I.G. Farben, which remains one of Germany's major industrial firms) replaced diesel fumes in the summer of 1942. With this innovation, seven hundred to eight hundred persons could be killed in four or five minutes. The bodies were mined for gold teeth, rings, and hair, then cremated. The ashes were heaped and used for fertilizer, and the clothes fumigated for reuse. The smoke of the cremation ovens could be seen from nearby towns and cities. The chief extermination camps were at Treblinka, Sobibor, Majdanek, and, of course, Auschwitz. Smaller extermination camps, where the work was done by firing squads, existed near major Jewish population cen-

ters of eastern Europe, such as Vilna, Riga, Minsk, Kovno, and Lvov.

Adolf Eichmann gave priority to the extermination of Polish Jewry because of the ease of transportation and because of the urging of Hans Frank, the governor of the region. The systematic evacuation of the Polish ghettos began in 1942. But Treblinka and Sobibor had to be abolished in late 1943 after prisoner rebellions and in the face of the advance of the Soviet army. The gassing of Jews continued until November 1944.

The concentration camps were also used as a source of slave labor for industry. I.G. Farben, Krupp, Thyssen, Flick, and Siemens (all functioning and prosperous German companies today), made up about 40 percent of their workforce from this source, with great benefits to their own profits. The camp authorities also enjoyed considerable profits from this labor, for the prisoners were given minimal food and virtually no medical care, cost little to maintain, and were simply worked to death. The average lifespan of a slave laborer was nine months, and the annual manpower turnover in some industries reached 300 percent. Eventually a conflict arose between the need for a cheap workforce made up of prisoners to support the war effort and the "Final Solution" mandating the rapid extermination of the prisoners. The solution was to institute a selection process carried out on the arrival of prisoner transports at the camps (most notoriously at Auschwitz), where the able-bodied were spared immediate gassing in order to be worked to death or gassed when no longer able to work.

As the Soviet army advanced from the East, the camps were evacuated; since no transport was provided, the prisoners were simply marched westward in long death marches with no provisions. Between the grueling marches and the conditions in the reception camps, about 250,000 prisoners died as a result of the evacuation.

used to instigate anti-Jewish riots. The Jewish population was concentrated into the ghettos that were by this point established, the first in Lodz, the largest in Warsaw. Jews were forced to wear an identifying badge, usually a yellow six-pointed star. The penalty for being found outside the ghetto was death. Jewish properties were appropriated, and Jews were subjected to forced labor, starvation, and brutality. The ghetto populations were put to work at enterprises related to the war effort, including the building of roads.

Within the ghettos, Jewish life was administered by Jewish councils, which were responsible to the Germans. To some extent, this arrangement continued the pre-emancipation pattern of Jewish semiautonomy and created an illusion of normalcy. In the early stages, Jews could receive aid from outside Jewish organizations, and those who worked at conscript labor received rations. In the larger, better organized ghettos, social institutions were maintained in the face of crowding, poverty, and disease. Some Jews even got economic concessions from the Germans in exchange for bribes and collaboration. But by late 1941, new restrictions had intensified hunger and disease, and the death rate rose dramatically.

When France was invaded in 1940, the Jews were expelled from occupied France to collaborationist Vichy France. The Vichy government in the South cooperated with the Germans in banning Jews from public activity and depriving non-French citizens of civil rights. German and Polish Jews who had fled to France were arrested. But even in occupied Paris, no ghetto was established, and though many Jews were transported, many others managed to evade the police with the help of friends.

In Holland, the persecution of the Jews roused popular anger, leading to a general strike, which had to be suppressed by the military. Even more supportive of the Jews were the Danes, who smuggled the entire Jewish community across the straits to Sweden. The Jews of Bulgaria were also spared because the people and the government refused to cooperate with the Germans.

As long as Italy remained unoccupied, its cooperation with its German ally was but spotty. Concentration camps were established in Italy, but the treatment of Jews in them was relatively humane. Everything changed, though, when Italy surrendered to the Allies in September 1943, at which point the northern part, which was where most of the Jewish population—including refugees from France and Yugoslavia—lived, fell under German control. The bulk of the Jewish population of Italy was now subject to be transported to death camps. But as in Paris, Holland, and Denmark, many Jews found non-Jews who were willing to protect them.

When the Germans invaded the Soviet Union in June 1941, training camps were established for action groups, which were to murder commissars, Jews, and gypsies in the newly occupied territories. The action groups generally worked in cooperation with the army, which was also instructed to add the killing of Jews to its military duties. Commando squads scoured eastern Europe, liquidating the Jewish populations (along with partisans and communists), generally by machine-gunning, but also by drowning or asphyxiation. Local police often participated in these actions as well. One of the most infamous of these killings occurred at Babi Yar, near Kiev, in September 1941, where Germans and Ukrainians murdered at least 34,000 Jews.

The decision to begin the systematic extermination of the Jews was taken at the end of 1941. In January 1942, representatives of various governmental and military agencies meeting in the Berlin suburb of Wannsee spelled out and coordinated the Final Solution, as the destruction of European Jewry was called in Nazi parlance. The goal was now to kill all the Jews in Europe, whose numbers were estimated at 11 million. All who were incapable of work were to be killed immediately; the others were to be worked to death in concentration camps. Poland was to be the extermination center.

The Jews of western Europe and the German Reich were shipped to the ghettos of Lodz, Riga, Minsk, and Kovno. In mid-1942, thousands were

LEFT: A Nazi firing squad in the Ukraine. The picture was taken through a window.

ABOVE: Jews carrying desecrated Torah scrolls out of a synagogue in Rovno, Ukraine, in 1944.

BELOW LEFT: Jewish men rounded up in the Ukraine early in the German occupation.

Majdanek, Sobibor, Dachau, and Buchenwald. Techniques of mass extermination were gradually refined, beginning with shootings and asphyxiation by diesel exhaust and culminating in the use of a pesticide administered in false showers in the camps. The Jews were crowded naked into the showers and gassed. Their gold teeth were removed before their bodies were cremated.

Meanwhile, in the ghettos, the starving and demoralized Jews were easily controlled by German and local troops; there was little resistance to the deportation orders even after their real purpose became generally known. The main uprising occurred in the Warsaw ghetto. It was precipitated by a clash that occurred in January 1943, when a group of young Jews awaiting transport fired on their guards and managed to escape. Encountering armed resistance and lack of cooperation in their search for the perpetrators, the Nazis decided to liquidate the ghetto. They began bombarding the ghetto on April 19, but the Jews were able to resist the Nazis for five weeks before being crushed. Although the struggle was hopeless from the beginning, it had great symbolic value as

sent to the area of Lublin and from there to extermination camps. The Jewish councils of the ghettos were ordered to deliver quotas of Jews for "resettlement." But by now, rumors of what really happened at these camps had begun to filter back to those still living in the ghettos.

New concentration camps were established and old ones expanded. The most notorious were those at Auschwitz, Bergen-Belsen, Treblinka, Mauthausen, a display of the dauntlessness of Jewish youth. Resistance groups were also formed in some other ghettos.

Despite the waning fortunes of the German troops in their war against the Allies, vast resources of money, personnel, equipment, and organizational ability were mobilized by Germany in its war against the Jews. And this is one war that Germany won, reducing the Jewish population by half and destroying Jewish communities and their culture. The most populous center of world Jewry had been turned into an appalling graveyard. European Jewish culture was completely broken.

Not only Ashkenazic Jewry suffered; the Jews of Salonica, one of the great centers of Sephardic Jewry, were exterminated at Auschwitz. The Jews of Greece and the Balkans, many of them Sephardim, were also exterminated at various camps.

After the Allies liberated the concentration camps at the war's end, the survivors who straggled back to their homes were often greeted upon their arrival by new pogroms. The devastated population of eastern Europe was turning its rage against its traditional scapegoat, the Jews.

Prisoners at the concentration camp at Dachau cheer their liberators, the U.S. 7th Army, on April 30, 1945.

CHAPTER NINE

ZIONISM AND THE BIRTH OF THE STATE OF ISRAEL

*T*o many nineteenth-century Jews contemplating the problem of their status as a barely tolerated foreign body, especially in eastern Europe, movements of national resurgence offered a potential solution. Perhaps, they reasoned, what had worked for the Serbs, the Bulgarians, and the Romanians would also work for the Jews.

The Enlightenment had not proved a satisfactory solution. Not only had it not led to the acceptance of the Jews of eastern Europe by the Slavic peoples, but in western Europe, where it had gradually achieved civil rights for the Jews, the result had actually been a diminution of Jewish identity. Nor had the Enlight-

enment put an end to anti-Semitism, even in the West. To many, it gradually became apparent that the only solution was to restore the Jewish people to the condition of a normal nation by creating a sovereign Jewish state, or at least an autonomous Jewish unit within a larger state.

As early as 1840, an American Jew, Mordecai Manuel Noah, proposed establishing a Jewish state on an island in the Niagara River in New York State under the name "Ararat," but the plan came to nothing. For most Jewish nationalist thinkers, the natural location for a Jewish state was the land of Israel. The traditional Jewish homeland was again in the hands

Bethlehem in the nineteenth century.

ABOVE: A greeting card for the Jewish New Year shows Polish Jews about to board the train for the first leg of their journey to Palestine. The legend at the lower left reads: "May you be inscribed for a good year!"

RIGHT: Theodor Herzl, founder of political Zionism.

of the crumbling Ottoman empire (after an interval under Egyptian control), which had already lost control of several of its territories to national revival movements. The hope for a Jewish state was expressed by writers in many different territories, including Moses Hess in Germany, who wrote *Rome and Jerusalem* (1862); Leon Pinsker in eastern Europe, who wrote *Autoemancipation* (1882); and by writers of the Hebrew press, including Eliezer Ben-Yehuda.

The emergence of nationalist Jewish organizations, collectively known as the Hibbat Zion ("Love of Zion") movement, was precipitated by the pogroms in Russia in 1881. Among them was the Bilu movement (its name is an acronym of the biblical exhortation "House of Jacob, go, let us go"), which actually emigrated to Palestine. In general, the Hibbat Zion movement had far greater success in eastern Europe—where Jews had had less success at and lower hopes for integration into general society and where the Jewish education and traditional life were very strong—than it did in Germany, where Jews were far more integrated into the dominant culture and economy and far less knowledgeable about their own culture.

But it was only through Theodor Herzl (1860–1904) that Zionism became an organized international movement. An unlikely candidate to be the force behind such a movement, Herzl was an assimilated Austrian-Jewish journalist with little knowledge of Judaism beyond his own experiences with anti-Semitism. He was also an admirer of France as a land of progress and enlightened ideas. As the Paris correspondent for a Viennese newspaper, he was shocked by the anti-Semitic outbursts that occurred there at the time of the Dreyfus trial. Alfred Dreyfus was a high-ranking Jewish officer in the French army who was accused of treason and convicted on the evidence of documents later proved to have been forged. The case exposed the widespread existence of anti-Semitism in the French army and among the public, and it became an international cause célèbre, especially with the intervention of the novelist Émile Zola. The trial and the public outcry led Herzl to look for possible solutions to the difficult situation of the Jews. In his book *The Jewish State* (1896), he argued that the only solution was the establishment of a Jewish state, and in *Old-New Land* (1902), he spoke prophetically about the social and technological achievements of which such a state would be capable.

In 1897, Herzl organized the First Zionist Congress in Switzerland, thereby creating the first Jew-

Nachum Sokolow (1859–1936), writer, longtime Zionist activist, and president of the World Zionist Organization from 1931 to 1935.

Jews of the pre-Zionist settlement in Palestine, praying at the Wailing Wall.

THE LANGUAGES OF THE JEWS: HEBREW

Hebrew is the only language that has ever been successfully revived after having fallen out of use as a spoken language. This feat was possible because, even though Hebrew was not spoken for about seventeen centuries, it was universally used by Jews in prayer and in study until the end of the nineteenth century. Since the study of classical books written in Hebrew (and in Aramaic, a closely related language) was traditionally considered a chief religious duty, a large percentage of world Jewry, probably the majority of males, was always somewhat literate in Hebrew, whether their spoken language was Arabic, Yiddish, Ladino, German, Polish, or any other.

Hebrew belongs to a group of languages known as the Semitic languages; the only other Semitic languages widely spoken today are Arabic and, to a much lesser extent, Amharic (the main language of Ethiopia). Aramaic is still spoken in a few communities of Christians, Muslims, and Jews in Syria, Turkey, and Kurdistan. These languages are quite different in structure from the languages of Europe. Most of their words have roots consisting of three consonants; vowels are used to modify the meanings of the basic roots according to certain fairly regular patterns. Originally, these languages had very few words in common with the Indo-European languages of Europe, but during the Hellenistic period, Hebrew absorbed many words of Greek origin. In modern times, many European loan words have entered both Hebrew and Arabic.

Ashkenazim and Sephardim had different traditions of pronunciation of Hebrew. Since the Ashkenazic Zionists pioneered the revival of Hebrew as a spoken language, they at first used the Ashkenazic pronunciation, but they soon shifted to Sephardic, which seemed to them to be more authentic since it was the prevailing pronunciation among the the Jews already present in Palestine. (We now know that neither system corresponds exactly to the way Hebrew was pronounced in biblical times.) In the course of a few generations, the Sephardic pronunciation was affected by the speech habits of eastern European speakers, so that Israeli pronunciation of Hebrew today can no longer be said to be truly Sephardic.

Many early Zionists refused to believe that it would be possible for a modern society to function using a language that had not been spoken in everyday life for centuries. Hebrew had no vocabulary for myriad everyday items and modern concepts. Herzl ridiculed the idea that someone someday might buy a railroad ticket in Hebrew.

The problem was solved by making use of the structure of the language itself to coin new words. The common Semitic root *rkb*, for example, widely used in the Bible, conveys the idea of riding. From this root, ancient Hebrew derived the verbs *rakhav* (to ride) and *hirkiv* (to mount someone on a horse; to graft); the participle *rokhev* ("rider"); and two different nouns meaning "chariot." In the late nineteenth century, a writer who wanted to use the word "train" in a magazine article managed to do so by combining this root with a common noun pattern, yielding the new word *rakevet*, and this word took hold among users of Hebrew for "train." The Hebrew word for "ticket," *kartis*, was adapted from an Aramaic word found in ancient Jewish sources. (It is actually a loan word from Greek, and distantly related to the English word "chart.") Verbs for "buy" and "sell," as well as numbers and designations for money, are all found in biblical Hebrew. Thus, what seemed to Herzl an unsolvable conundrum—how to say "I bought a railroad ticket to Haifa"—became the simple, everyday sentence *"qaniti kartis rakevet lehefa."*

Even with the new coinages, new speakers of Hebrew sometimes tended to fall back on words from their native languages, giving these words a Hebrew pronunciation. Thus, for many years the word *éxel* was used in Hebrew for the axle of a car or truck, even though a perfectly good Hebrew word exists. Sometimes a newly coined Hebrew word manages to oust the foreign word (as *meda*, coined in the 1960s, has replaced the formerly common word *informatsya* for "information"). Sometimes it does not, and the foreign word becomes an accepted loan word in Hebrew (like *televisya* for television, which has never yielded to the word *sikayon*, coined in the 1950s).

In 1882, Hebrew had one native speaker; he was Itamar Ben Avi, the son of Eliezer Ben-Yehuda. Today, Hebrew has about three million native speakers, many of whom are not even Jewish. The language has changed rapidly in the last hundred years, and it is now fully capable of expressing anything a modern person needs to say. It has served several genera-

tions of speakers as a native language, used not out of ideological principle, but simply as a vehicle for the expression of ordinary peoples' deepest feelings and most routine activities.

The result of this revival has been a burst of literary creativity unparalleled in Jewish history. Fiction and poetry have poured out of Israel in the generation since the establishment of the state, and some of this new Jewish literature has begun to find its way into English and other European languages. A Hebrew novelist has won the Nobel Prize; poems by Yehuda Amichai have appeared in the New York subways; the fiction of Amos Oz, A.B. Yehoshua, and David Grossman is regularly reviewed in American newspapers. Even a murder mystery by Batya Gur can be bought in American bookstores.

Chart showing the relationship between the Greek, Egyptian Hieratic, and Phoenician alphabets. The Phoenician alphabet was used for Hebrew until the Second Commonwealth period. It was revived briefly by Bar Kochba.

ish organization to offer an independent Jewish political plan. The outcome was the "Basel Program," which stated, "Zionism aspires to the securing of a national home for the Jewish people in Palestine, guaranteed by public law." But some scoffed at Herzl's political programs as unrealistic, and others demanded more concentration on cultural activity. In despair of getting the sanction of the Ottoman sultan to establish the Jewish state in Palestine, Herzl entered into negotiations with Great Britain to permit a Jewish settlement in Uganda. As a result, opposition to his leadership intensified. Great Britain ultimately withdrew from the negotiations, and Herzl again embraced the dream of a Jewish state in Palestine.

Meanwhile, in Palestine itself, the Bilu immigrants, arriving in 1882, had settled in alongside the various Jewish populations that had been present since the Ottoman conquest in the fifteenth century: descendants of the Sephardic refugees who had undergone the expulsion from Spain, descendants of more recent immigrants from the Middle Eastern countries, and descendants of various European pietistic groups who had settled in Palestine during the eighteenth and early nineteenth centuries. The pre-Zionist Jewish population had grown to such a point that in 1860, Jews began to build new quarters—the neighborhoods that today make up the city's downtown—outside the walls of Jerusalem. Although life still followed traditional religious and economic patterns, there was some interest in establishing agricultural settlements, especially after the Alliance Israélite Universelle founded an agricultural school in 1870.

The Bilu immigrants, who made up the first wave of modern Jewish immigration, actually arrived with the intention of establishing agricultural colonies as the basis of the Jewish settlement and as the main step toward the return of all Jews to Palestine. Despite their idealism, though, they did not have the know-how to build successful settlements. They would certainly have foundered had it not been for extensive financial support by Baron Edmond de Rothschild.

Eliezer Ben-Yehuda, who revived Hebrew as a spoken language.

This period of the first modern settlement saw the beginnings of an outstanding cultural achievement of the Jewish people in modern times—the revival of Hebrew as a spoken language. We have already seen that, although Hebrew had ceased to be spoken during the first century A.D., it was used in rabbinic writing throughout the course of Jewish history. Given the central role of the study of books in Jewish religious ideology and practice, Hebrew literacy was widespread. And given the role of national languages in the rise of the various nationalist movements of the age, Jewish intellectuals, especially in eastern Europe, turned naturally to Hebrew. By the late eighteenth century, Jewish writers had already begun using Hebrew as a vehicle for educating the eastern European masses in such modern subjects as mathematics, science, and geography; soon, Hebrew was being used for poetry and, by the mid-nineteenth century, for fiction.

The catalyst of the Hebrew movement was Eliezer Ben-Yehuda (1858–1922), who, inspired by the struggle of the Balkan nations for liberation, committed his life to struggle for the restoration of the Jewish people to its historic land and language. In 1881, he moved to Palestine and soon thereafter began to campaign for the revival of Hebrew, starting with his wife, to whom he announced on their arrival that from now on he would communicate with her only in that language. He adopted the Sephardic pronunciation, which was widely used in Palestine and which remains the basis of spoken Hebrew today. He introduced Hebrew as the language of some of the instruction in the Alliance school in Jerusalem, and he published newspapers and periodicals dealing with both specifically Jewish and general topics, coining Hebrew words as needed. After his release from imprisonment on a false charge of sedition, he devoted most of his energies to the compilation of a massive, seventeen-volume historical dictionary of Hebrew. Part of this work was published in his lifetime, and part completed after his death; the last volumes appeared in 1959. He also founded and chaired the Hebrew Language Committee, the forerunner of the

TOP: Early Jewish agricultural settlements in Palestine.

ABOVE: In the Jordan Valley, a Jewish settler harvests tomatoes.

present-day Hebrew Language Academy, which, like the French *Académie Française*, is the arbiter of linguistic questions for the State of Israel.

Although Hebrew had not been spoken in everyday life for centuries, it was a natural bridge between the mostly Sephardic population of Palestine and the increasing numbers of Ashkenazim who began to arrive with the Biluim. Ben-Yehuda's efforts were successful, and Hebrew was accepted—albeit in the face of considerable debate and dissension— as the language of the nascent Jewish homeland.

Early Jewish agricultural settlement in Palestine.

The revival of Hebrew was an event without parallel in world history.

The Kishinev pogrom in Russia in 1903 and the failure of the 1905 Russian revolution precipitated a resurgence of immigration to Palestine that lasted for ten years. The immigrants of this second wave were mostly intellectuals, idealistic pioneers devoted to socialism. Their intellectual hero was A. D. Gordon, who developed the idea of the beneficial power of labor and the return to nature in regenerating the Jewish people. It was these immigrants who created the characteristic agricultural institutions of Israel: the collective settlement (*kibbutz*) and the cooperative settlement (*moshav*). They were also committed to Hebrew as the everyday language of the Jews. In 1909, they laid the foundations of Tel Aviv, the first all-Jewish city in Palestine and today the metropolis of Israel.

The increase of Jewish population and the expansion of Jewish agricultural settlements caused a corresponding intensification of opposition by local Arabs. This opposition increased after the Turkish revolution in 1908, which led to the establishment of an organized Arab nationalist movement. Security became a problem for the Jewish settlements.

During World War I, the Turkish governor of Palestine, Jamal Pasha, carried out extensive arrests and ordered the banishment of many of the Jewish settlers. When a Jewish espionage outfit working for the British was uncovered, he used it as a pretext for the persecution of Jewish settlements, even those who opposed the espionage. Thus, when the British General Allenby entered Jerusalem in December 1917, he was welcomed by the Jews.

Zionist leaders in England, hoping for a British victory over Turkey, did their best to persuade the British government to recognize the rights of the Jewish people in Palestine after the liberation of the country; to permit free immigration; and to recognize the legal status of Zionist institutions there. As mentioned in chapter six, a Jewish legion composed of Palestinian Jews was formed to fight on behalf of the Allies. These efforts culminated in the formal declaration by British Foreign Secretary Lord Balfour in 1917 that the British government "view with favour the establishment in Palestine of a national home for the Jewish people and would use their best endeavours to facilitate the achievement of this object."

The postwar period saw a third wave of Jewish immigration, consisting of members of the Pioneer movement, which also stressed agricultural and manual labor and the fostering of Hebrew language and culture. This period saw intense negotiations as European Zionist leaders and the British government discussed the future of the mandate for Palestine that Britain expected to obtain from the newly formed League of Nations, and the European Zionist leaders negotiated with Abdallah, the son of Sherif Hussein of Mecca, in the hope of obtaining the cooperation of the latter. (Hussein was an Arabian leader whom the British had encouraged to revolt against the Turks, promising him in return to recognize him as king of western Arabia.) By this time, the British Zionists, headed by Chaim Weizmann, were the international leaders of the movement, working closely with American Zionists headed by Supreme Court Justice Louis Brandeis.

TOP LEFT: Lord Arthur Balfour (1848–1930).

LEFT: Chaim Weizmann (1874–1952) in 1940.

TOP: A British patrol stopping and searching an Arab.

ABOVE: A crowd of Arabs listening to a speech by the Arab nationalist leader Jamal Effendi al-Husseini outside the Tomb of David on Mount Zion in 1934.

During this long period of negotiations, there were Arab attacks on Jewish settlements, which led the British to halt Jewish immigration briefly. Jewish battalions were formed in response, but the British authorities would not permit them to operate, so they were disbanded. This experience showed Jewish leaders that it would be necessary to create an independent but clandestine military force to defend settlers from Arab attacks.

As a result of the riots, the territory of Palestine east of the Jordan was separated and placed under Arab control in 1921; on his visit to the area, Winston Churchill, then colonial secretary, granted rule of this region, known as Transjordan, to the emir Abdullah. But Arab objections to the Jewish presence in western Palestine grew ever stronger and were exacerbated by the appointment of an extreme Arab nationalist, Amin al-Husseini, as mufti (Muslim religious authority) of Jerusalem.

Britain received the mandate over Palestine officially in 1922. At that time, Palestine was considered to include the inhabited territory on both sides of the Jordan. The intention of the mandate was to implement the Balfour declaration. It envisioned the establishment of a Jewish national home, and for this purpose established the Jewish Agency, which was to cooperate with the British administration in bringing about this goal. The organization was supposed to encourage Jewish immigration and settlement, while at the same time guaranteeing the rights of others groups in the territory.

During the 1920s, the Jewish institutions of Palestine, such as the Haganah (Defense Organization), the Histadrut (General Federation of Hebrew Workers), and the Hebrew University, came into being, and Arab opposition to the Jewish presence intensified. In 1929, there arose serious riots, incited partly by the inflammatory propaganda of the mufti, which included murderous attacks in Jerusalem, Safed, and especially Hebron. In an effort to appease the Arabs, the British temporarily put a stop to Jewish immigration. Within the Jewish community, the decade also saw the growth of a serious right-wing movement,

the Revisionists, headed by Vladimir Jabotinsky. The Revisionists opposed the labor groups, which were dominated by the Mapai party and its leader, David Ben-Gurion. Tension between the two groups became severe during the course of the 1930s. One outcome was the secession of Revisionists from the Haganah and the creation of an independent Revisionist military force, the Irgun.

The persecutions of Jews in Europe during the 1930s resulted in increased immigration to Palestine and therefore an increased amount of tension between Jews and Arabs. These tensions were exacerbated by the popularity of Nazism with Arab nationalists. An Arab Higher Commission was formed, and Arab military groups began sabotage operations against Jewish settlements. A general Arab strike in 1936 lasted six months and led the

Vladimir Jabotinsky (1880–1940), leader of the New Zionist Organization, the ancestor of Israel's nationalist Likud party.

TOP: New immigrants arriving at the port of Haifa in the 1930s. The sign says "Baggage Inspection" in Hebrew and Arabic.

ABOVE: British soldiers man a barricade as anti-Jewish riots by Arabs necessitate the declaration of martial law.

immigration yet again. More important, the British decided that the national aspirations of Jews and Arabs were irreconcilable and that the territory should again be partitioned.

The new plan called for the creation of a Jewish state that would comprise the coastal strip, Galilee, and Jezreel Valley; an Arab state that would comprise the central hill country and the Negev; and a British enclave that would include Jerusalem, Jaffa, and several other cities. The Jews were divided as to whether they should support the plan. While Labor was mostly in favor, Revisionists were strongly opposed. The Arabs rejected the proposal completely, and in 1937 resolved upon armed struggle.

With all this opposition, the British soon realized that the plan could not be implemented. In 1939, they issued the infamous White Paper, severely restricting Jewish immigration to Palestine and in effect retracting the Balfour declaration. While plans and pronouncements came and went, Arab attacks on Jewish settlements became increasingly militarized, and the Jewish settlers increasingly demoralized, until the entire issue was thrown into the background by World War II.

Although the Palestinian Jews cooperated with the British during the war, providing several fighting forces, relations between the Jews and the British government continued to deteriorate after the German forces in Libya were defeated in 1942. Restrictions were imposed on Jews obtaining arms, and attempts of refugees from Europe to enter Palestine were cruelly rejected. Britain came to appear more and more as the enemy. As a result, the Revisionists in effect declared war on the Mandatory government and embarked on a program of sabotage and assassination. These actions were rejected by the official Jewish institutions of Palestine, which then cooperated with the British in bringing about arrests. This cooperation in turn exacerbated tensions among the Jewish settlers.

Even the presence of tens of thousands of Jewish refugees in Europe after the war did not soften British immigration policy. A real struggle began as ramshackle boats laden with refugees began to arrive from Europe and were sent back by the British. The Palestinian leadership was at this point unified in its opposition to British policy and attempted to demonstrate by military means that the British could no longer control the country. A state of warfare came into being between Britain and the Jews. The climax was the arrest of thousands of Jews in June 1946 and the confiscation of Jewish arms. In retalia-

ABOVE: Arab Legion gun crews operating Bren guns during training in Transjordan, 1948.

LEFT: Workers repair the Tegart wall on the Palestinian-Syrian border, damaged by anti-Jewish Arab raiders in 1938.

ABOVE: The Rex Cinema in Jerusalem burning, having been set on fire in December 1947 during rioting over the U.N. vote to partition Palestine.

ABOVE LEFT: British troops being evacuated from Palestine in May 1948, as the British Mandate ends.

LEFT: The end of the British Mandate in Palestine: High Commissioner Sir Alan Gordon Cunningham's convoy leaves Jerusalem on May 14, 1948.

Israel's first prime minister was born David Gruen in 1886 in Russian Poland to a Zionist family, and in his childhood was involved with labor Zionism. At age twenty, he settled in Palestine and became active in a Marxist Zionist organization. He soon became convinced that true Zionism could only mean settling in the land of Israel, that life in Israel must be based on the collectivist principles of the kibbutz movement, and that Hebrew must become the language of public life in the Jewish state. In 1910, he adopted the Hebrew name Ben-Gurion and worked with Izhak Ben-Zvi (who later became the second president of Israel) to organize the Jews of Turkey for Jewish autonomy in Palestine; in Turkey, this activity got him arrested. In 1921, he became one of the leaders of the Histadrut, the Jewish labor organization in Palestine, which he hoped to use as a force for encouraging immigration, the advancement of labor, and his collectivist ideals. This led to the creation of a strong opposition, the Revisionist movement, led by Vladimir Jabotinsky. But during the 1930s, Labor tended to dominate both the World Zionist Organization and the Jewish Agency. Ben-Gurion was chairman of the Jewish Agency from 1935 to 1948.

Ben-Gurion opposed Britain's restrictive immigration policies of the late 1930s; but during World War II, he insisted on curbing violence against the British, and even cooperated with the British in arresting members of right-wing groups. When, after World War II, it became clear that Britain would not soften these policies, he led the political struggle and authorized sabotage activities against British authorities in Palestine. He also strengthened the Haganah, the Jewish defense force, in preparation for war with the Arabs of the region.

In the War of Independence, Ben-Gurion forged various Jewish military organizations into a single Jewish army, sometimes in the face of considerable opposition. Immediately on the termination of the British mandate, he proclaimed the independence of the state of Israel. He became provisional prime minister and minister of defense, and after the first elections, formed the first coalition government as prime minister. He resigned in 1954 and joined a kibbutz in the Negev, hoping to set an example for young people.

In 1955, he returned to government, first as minister of defense under Prime Minister Moshe Sharett, then as prime minister and minister of defense. He engaged with France and Britain in planning the Sinai campaign of 1956, and he negotiated with Germany for economic and military aid. He retired again in 1961 and was replaced by Levi Eshkol. In 1965, he formed a new political party, but did not receive wide support. He was elected to the Knesset (the Israeli Parliament), where he continued to serve until his final resignation in 1970. He died in 1973.

Ben-Gurion was colorful, impulsive, and strong-willed to the point of being dogmatic. He was a powerful public speaker. His interests were wide-ranging, including biblical studies, Buddhism, and philosophy. He was involved in many controversies, some of which left him looking less than dignified. But as a key figure in the creation of the Jewish state and as one of its first and most influential leaders, he is and always will be revered as a figure of almost mythical proportions in the history of the Jewish people.

David Ben-Gurion and an Israeli official, who holds Israel's Declaration of Independence.

TOP: The King David Hotel, site of British mandatory offices, after it was partially blown up by Jewish terrorists in 1946.

ABOVE: Rescue workers carry out victims of the explosion.

tion, the Irgun blew up the King David Hotel in Jerusalem, where many government agencies had their offices. Opposed by the majority of the Jewish leadership, this action put an end to cooperation between the Jewish right and left. The British authorities responded with mass arrests and by setting up detention camps in Cyprus for the illegal immigrants, who had only recently been released from the German death camps. Arrests and executions of Jewish leaders were increased in an attempt to break the spirit of the Jews. But instead, these actions only strengthened their fighting spirit, bringing the Jews together in opposition against Britain.

Nevertheless, basic policy differences did continue to exist between the main Jewish institutions, governed by the Jewish Agency, and the Revisionists. By the end of 1946, the latter had embarked on a campaign of terror against the British that was rejected by the Jewish Agency. The Jewish officials were opposed to the Revisionist campaign not only on moral and tactical grounds, but also because the Revisionists' independent actions undermined the authority of the agency.

Exasperated by its inability to reconcile the competing interests of Jews and Arabs, Britain now turned the problem over to the United Nations. On November 29, 1947, the General Assembly voted to partition Palestine into two states; the motion was supported by both the United States and, unexpectedly, by the Soviet Union. The Arabs announced that they would forcibly resist partition (even though they had already been granted sovereignty over Transjordan and even though the new partition plan provided for an Arab state on the west bank), and Britain announced that it would not cooperate in carrying out the plan. Thus, implementation was left to the Jews of Palestine and world Jewry. The date for the British withdrawal from Palestine was set for May 15, 1948. On Friday, May 14, in Tel Aviv, David Ben-Gurion—head of the Jewish Agency—proclaimed the establishment of a Jewish state in Palestine, to be known as the State of Israel. But the Israeli War of Independence had already begun.

CHAPTER TEN

JEWISH LIFE AFTER 1948

ISRAEL

*I*srael's war for independence was fought not against the colonial power from which it sought liberation but against the neighbors who resented its presence and coveted its territory. The war began at the time of the United Nations' vote to partition Palestine, six months before the official end of the British Mandate. During the transition of government, the British authorities held to a policy of non-cooperation and did nothing to prevent Arab attacks. On the morning following the proclamation of the Jewish state, the armies of the neighboring states—Jordan, Iraq, Syria, Lebanon, and Egypt—invaded Israel with some support from Saudi Arabia and Yemen. In their sheer numbers and geographical advantage, these forces of opposition seemed invincible. Most observers assumed that the war against the poorly armed and scattered Jewish settlements would soon be over.

It was soon over, but with unexpected results. By the final cease-fire, in January 1949, the new Israel Defense Force had beaten back the attackers and had obtained control of the Galilee, the coastal strip, the Negev, the road to Jerusalem, and the western part of Jerusalem itself, which was more territory than the partition plan had envisioned. Jordan had expanded its territory by seizing the central hill country west of the Jordan River (today generally known as the West Bank) and the eastern part of Jerusalem, including the historic part within the Ottoman walls.

Much of the Arab population in the territories secured by Israel had fled, certain that they would return soon with victorious Arab troops to recover their homes and orchards. Other Arabs were expelled. There was at least one major atrocity, when the villagers of Deir Yassin were slaughtered, resulting in the mass flight of Arabs from the region. Jordan and the other neighboring countries refused to absorb the Arab refugees. Instead, they placed them in camps that were intended to be temporary, but that turned into long-lasting impoverished settlements where three and even four generations of Palestinian Arabs incubated their rage against Israel.

The first general elections were held in January 1949, establishing the Israeli parliament, called the Knesset, which in turn elected a government headed by David Ben-Gurion as prime minister and the aged Chaim Weizmann as president. The Knesset sat

OPPOSITE: American Labor Zionists celebrating the United Nations' decision to partition Palestine, November 30, 1947.

ABOVE: On January 28, 1949 at the Israeli Constitutional Assembly election, David Ben-Gurion casts his vote.

in Jerusalem, the obvious capital of the Jewish state, though some countries (including the United States), refused to accept Jerusalem as the capital, presumably because the now-superseded partition plan had envisioned making Jerusalem an international city.

The Knesset soon enacted the Law of Return, permitting any Jew immigrating to Israel to claim automatic Israeli citizenship upon arrival. And immigrants were arriving in great numbers. With the gates now open, Israel was flooded with refugees from the Arab lands and Europe. Many came from premodern regions and were unfamiliar with the predominantly European and technologically advanced society that they had now joined. The population was desperately needed, but its absorption presented enormous economic and social problems for the new state.

The Arab nations had lost the war, but they refused to concede peace. They would not sit with the Israeli representatives at the armistice negotiations, and when the war was over, they instituted a boycott, refusing to do business with any shipping line that called at Israeli ports or any company that traded with Israel. Airplanes to and from Israel were not allowed to fly over the surrounding Arab territories, and no one bearing an Israeli visa could enter the Arab countries. The Suez Canal was closed to Israel, and ships that had passed through it were prevented by Egypt from calling at Israel's southern port of Eilat. Jewish shrines in Jerusalem's old city were desecrated and access to them blocked to Jews. Needless to say, the Arab countries agreed not to recognize Israel; for decades, Arabic newspapers would avoid calling the country by name, referring to it instead as "the Zionist entity." Jordan and Egypt also kept up the war by supporting groups of guerrillas (known as *fedaiyin* in Arabic) who constantly infiltrated Israel to make unexpected and demoralizing attacks wherever they could.

In the 1950s, the Middle East became caught up in the Cold War. Encouraged by the Soviet Union,

Egypt seized the Suez Canal from Britain and France; and the armies of Syria, Jordan, and Egypt, unified under Egyptian command, massed in the Sinai. In order to recover the canal, France entered into a conspiracy with Britain and Israel. In accordance with the plan, Israel attacked the Sinai on October 29, 1956, and within a week destroyed the Egyptian army, capturing all of Sinai in the process. On October 31, Britain and France entered Port Said, ostensibly to separate the fighting parties, but actually to seize the canal. World outcry against all three parties was instantaneous and intense. With no political support, Israel was forced to abandon the Sinai in return for weak U.N. guarantees to supervise the Israeli-Egyptian border.

Ten years of consolidation followed. There was no real peace with the neighboring Arab states, but there was sufficient calm to allow Israel to absorb its immigrants, develop its economy, and emerge from the rationing and privation of its first decade as a nation. One interesting development of the period was the formation of relations with Germany. In 1959, an agreement was reached by which Germany invested large amounts of money in Israel as compensation for material damage caused to Jews during the persecutions. This money provided a big boost to Israel's economy, but the Israeli public was torn about accepting it, for many who had actually lived through the horrible events that Germany perpetrated wanted nothing to do with German blood-money. Ben-Gurion, however, saw it as a duty to restore to the Jewish people whatever could be restored them.

Soon thereafter, the Israeli secret police caught in Argentina a former high official of the German government, Adolf Eichmann, who had been involved on a national level in planning and executing the program for the extermination of the Jews. His trial in Jerusalem was used as an opportunity to educate the world about the crimes committed by Germany against the Jews. Witness after witness testified over a period of months about what they had endured

LEFT: Adolf Eichmann (1906–1962), the Gestapo officer responsible for organizing the mass murder of Jews by Germany in World War II.

BELOW: Eichmann, on trial in Jerusalem in 1961, was protected behind a specially designed partition.

at the hands of this man and his countrymen. Eichmann was hanged in 1962, the only person ever executed under Israeli law.

Israel's position in the Middle East was radically changed by the war that broke out in 1967. Syria and Egypt, encouraged by Russia, claimed that Israel was mobilizing on its northern and southern borders in preparation for a major offensive. Egypt's President Nasser, certain that he would now be able to settle his accounts with Israel from the Sinai campaign, ordered the removal of the United Nations Emergency Force from the Israeli-Egyptian border and blocked the shipping route to Eilat. Equally certain of an Egyptian victory, King Hussein of Jordan put his army under Egyptian command. The tension mounted for weeks in anticipation of the inevitable Arab attack.

But Israel acted first. Rapidly mobilizing its army, composed almost entirely of ordinary citizens, Israel preempted the attack and struck on June 5, 1967, demolishing, in only a few hours, Egypt's air force before the planes had even gotten into the air. The Israeli army then entered the Sinai, reaching the Suez Canal in just a few days. When King Hussein made the fatal error of attacking Jerusalem, Israel quickly responded by taking the Old City, East Jerusalem, and the entire West Bank, which Jordan had occupied at the time of Israel's war of independence. Syria lost the Golan Heights, from which it had frequently attacked Israel's northern settlements, and the Israeli army reached within striking distance of Damascus before the war was over. Only six days had passed. Israel quickly asserted sovereignty over the united city of Jerusalem, but left the fate of the occupied territories to be determined by negotiations that it expected would follow.

Israel had solved the immediate problem of an attack by Syria and Egypt—crippling their armies in the process—but it had not solved its overall political problem. The Arab countries still refused to accept Israel's existence. They demanded that Israel withdraw to the borders of the 1947 partition plan, but they would not agree to sign peace treaties based on those borders. Thus, fighting between Israel and Egypt went on intermittently until 1972, with the Egyptian forces constantly being restocked by the Soviet Union.

Israeli soldiers at leisure during the 1967 Arab-Israeli war.

Border tensions continued, aggravated by the emergence of organized Arab terrorism, which had begun with the founding of the Palestine Liberation Organization in 1964. After being violently expelled from Jordan in 1970, the PLO, an umbrella of Arab organizations established with the aim of working for the destruction of Israel, took up headquarters in Lebanon and commenced attacks on northern Israel. But the PLO did not limit its activities to Israeli territory, performing killings—including the cold-blooded murder of eleven Israeli athletes at the 1972 Olympics in Munich—hijackings, and kidnappings worldwide. Nonetheless, Israeli society thrived, enjoying an influx of immigrants from the Soviet Union, good relations with the European Common Market as well as many individual countries, and excellent tourism. After the Six-Day War, nobody took the military power of the Arab states very seriously.

But in 1973, Israel was taken by surprise. On Yom Kippur, which fell on October 6 that year, Egypt and Syria made a coordinated attack. Yom Kippur is the one religious holiday that is taken seriously even by secular Jews; it is a day when everything in Israel closes down. Israel had been aware of some suspicious movements in the neighboring countries, but its military intelligence provided only a few hours' notice of the attack. Mobilization began only four hours in advance, and men being called into service had to be tracked down in synagogues all over the country. This was the nearest Israel had come to disaster since independence.

Even with their late start, the Israelis succeeded in driving the Syrians back across the 1967 line in five days. The position in Egypt, which was constantly being resupplied by the Soviet Union, was more tenuous until Israel received help from the United States in the form of a shipment of war planes. On October 15, the Israelis crossed the Suez Canal. By the time the cease-fire was called, the Israeli army was only seventy miles (113km) from Cairo.

This war was followed by a dark time for Israel. Although from a purely military standpoint Israel

ABOVE: The Olympic stadium with the flags of some participating nations at half-mast during a memorial service for the slain athletes.

LEFT: Above, an Arab "Black September" terrorist in a face mask peers from the balcony of the Israeli Olympic squad's headquarters, which the terrorists had raided. Below, a member of the International Olympic Committee talks with one of the guerrillas.

BELOW: The eleven Israelis killed by Arab terrorists at the 1972 Olympics in Munich.

had actually won the war, it had lost the self-confidence generated by the Six-Day War only six years earlier. The reputations and careers of some of its most distinguished leaders were ruined or at least tarnished, and the jaunty optimism of Israel's early years had been lost. Could the state be depended upon to protect its citizens? Why did Israel keep winning wars without ever gaining the political advantages that ordinarily accrue to victors? Soon after the war, demoralization and anger intensified when PLO terrorists infiltrated the northern towns of Kiryat Shmonah and Maalot.

Prime Minister Golda Meir in 1973, at the time of Israel's twenty-fifth anniversary.

Public opinion was lifted somewhat by one Israeli success, which recalled the gallant heroism of Israel's struggle for independence. This was the rescue of Jewish hostages from a plane hijacked by PLO members and taken to Entebbe, Uganda. When the terrorists released everyone except the Jewish passengers, Israel decided that it had to act. In a brilliantly prepared raid, Israeli commandos succeeded in rescuing the hostages.

But most Israelis were ready for change. In the elections of 1977, they threw aside the Labor party, which had dominated the state throughout its entire history, and replaced it with Likud (the political party descended from the pre-state Revisionist Zionists). The party's head, Menachem Begin, became prime minister.

When Begin took office, he was invited by American president Jimmy Carter to open negotia-

tions with the Arabs under American supervision. After a few months of negotiations, Egyptian president Sadat took Israel by surprise, announcing his willingness to visit Israel and address the Knesset. The ceremonial reception of President Sadat in Israel in November 1977 was one of the two or three most emotional moments in Israeli history. Sadat and Begin were taking enormous risks with the futures of both their countries and their own careers. But everyone recognized the particular heroism of Sadat, who was the only Arab public figure ever to have reached out to Israel to make peace.

The negotiations were difficult, though, for Egypt expected Israel to withdraw from the West Bank, which hard-liner Begin considered an integral part of historic Israel. In 1978, President Carter broke the impasse by convening a conference at Camp David. By March 1979, an agreement was reached, thanks largely to continual pressure from President Carter. Israel agreed to return the Sinai to Egypt in exchange for a peace treaty and normalized relations. Although the arrangement was bitterly opposed by many on Israel's right—especially by the settlers in Yamit, an Israeli town in the Sinai—the entire Sinai was again in Egyptian hands on April 25, 1982. Thus, Israel and Egypt arrived at peace, which has been maintained through all vicissitudes down to the present.

Unfortunately, President Sadat became a victim of the peace process for which he had been so largely responsible. In October 1981, he was assassinated by a Muslim fanatic and thus did not live to see the completion of the return of the Sinai.

Less than a year later, Israel was at war again, this time in Lebanon. The Lebanese border had traditionally been a quiet one, and Lebanon had long seemed amenable to making peace with Israel. But when the PLO, expelled from Jordan, made Lebanon its headquarters, Syria attempted to intervene in the country, resulting in a civil war that lasted through most of the 1970s and fragmented the country's political structure. Supplied by the Soviet Union, the PLO continued to bombard settlements in northern Israel from Lebanon until, in 1982, Israel decided to push the PLO back out of striking distance. With the immediate objective achieved in short order, Israel continued her advance into Lebanon, seizing PLO arms, eliminating Syrian positions, and besieging the PLO in Beirut. The war ended up lasting much longer than predicted, though. It was unpopular at home and was condemned internationally, particularly after the massacre of Palestinians in two Lebanese villages by Lebanese troops, which, it was generally believed, the Israeli troops ought to have prevented. Worst of all, the incursion into Lebanon cost many Israelis their lives without changing the situation it was intended to remedy, for although Lebanon was prepared to make peace with Israel, Syrian troops and the PLO, both implacably hostile to Israel, remained in the territory; consequently, Israel refused to with-

TOP: Egyptian president Anwar Sadat reviewing the Israeli honor guard on his arrival at Ben-Gurion Airport on November 19, 1977.

ABOVE: Israeli prime minister Menachem Begin and Egyptian president Anwar Sadat at the Knesset (Parliament), November 20, 1977.

TOP: United States president Jimmy Carter, Egyptian president Anwar Sadat, and Israeli prime minister Menachem Begin clasping hands at the White House in 1979, following the signing of the Israeli-Egyptian peace treaty.

ABOVE: The funeral of Egyptian president Anwar Sadat in 1981.

draw from the security zone it had established in the south of Lebanon. Attacks by these forces on northern Israel and on the security zone were to continue throughout the 1980s, especially with the growth of an Islamic fundamentalist movement, the Hezbullah, in Lebanon. Broken both by the failure in Lebanon

and by the death of his wife in 1983, Begin resigned his office and retired into obscurity that same year.

Tensions between Israel and the Arabs of the occupied territories continued to increase during the 1980s. Years of occupation had created a strong sense of Palestinian identity among these people, who had not had a strong and distinctive national identity before the occupation. The vast majority felt that their interests were best represented by the PLO, headed then by Yasir Arafat. Beginning in 1987, systematic demonstrations and strikes in the occupied territories and in Jerusalem expressed Palestinian rage against Israel, amounting to a popular uprising that came to be known as the intifada. Israeli attempts to suppress this disturbance led, inevitably, to increased violence.

A dramatic change occurred in 1988 when King Hussein of Jordan relinquished his claims to the West Bank, at which point the PLO declared the establishment of an independent Palestinian state. Israel, headed at the time by an even more rigid Revisionist, Prime Minister Itzhak Shamir, refused to negotiate with the PLO on account of its professed goal of destroying Israel; though the PLO indicated indirectly a willingness to concede Israel's legitimacy, it refused to rescind the part of its constitution that called for Israel's destruction, which was the reason for the PLO's establishment in the first place. Although Shamir made several proposals for resolving the problem of the occupied territories, his government actually exacerbated the situation by supporting the construction of new Jewish settlements in the West Bank, which the Palestinian Arabs now viewed as their country.

Hard pressed by the United States, Israel participated formally in negotiations with various Arab states, but no progress could be made under the Shamir government, which would not deal with the PLO or halt new construction in the West Bank. A much-publicized conference between representatives of Israel and several Arab states held in Madrid in 1991 did not actually move the process along at all. The return of the Labor party to power in 1992, under Prime Minister Yitzhak Rabin, boded greater flexibility in the Israeli positions. But the intifada continued, leading to Israeli punitive actions and tighter security measures, such as curfews, exiling terrorists, demolishing houses that harbored terrorists, and closing the borders through which terrorists routinely infiltrated Israel from the occupied territories. These measures, the minimum that a responsible government could do to protect its public, were routinely condemned by international bodies. In such an atmosphere of constant crisis, neither side could sit down with the other to discuss a long-term settlement. One conference after another was broken off with no progress made.

Thus, the world was taken by surprise when the announcement was made that Israel and the PLO had for some time been engaged in secret negotiations in Norway that had culminated in an agreement of mutual recognition and the formulation of a Declaration of Principles. The agreement envisioned Israel's gradual concession of control over the West Bank and Gaza to the PLO. At a moving ceremony held in Washington on the lawn of the White House on September 13, 1993, the agreement was formalized, and Arafat and Rabin shook hands in public. The following year, the Gaza Strip and the area around Jericho came officially under PLO control.

The gesture on the White House lawn seemed to symbolize the beginning of an unstoppable motion toward resolution. It did not, however, spell the end of the problem, for on both sides there were, and continue to be, forces opposed to resolution. Many on both sides had been hardened by the long conflict to the point that they would not trust the other side, and those who had personally suffered the deaths of parents and children could not forgive and forget. But more dismaying was the symmetrical presence on both sides of large groups who were opposed to a settlement on principle and who actually embraced conflict.

On the Arab side were the religious extremists, Muslim fundamentalists who saw the presence of a Jewish state on formerly Muslim-ruled territory as an offense to Islam itself, and who were willing not only to kill Jews, but also to die themselves as martyrs in order to fight it. These movements, financed partly by Iran and other countries, emerged in the 1980s as a counterforce to the PLO, which many Palestinian Arabs had come to view as a collaborationist agency because of its willingness to deal with Israel. One such extremist movement is Hammas. Hammas also attracted some Palestinian Arabs who were dissatisfied with Arafat's management of Palestinian affairs but were unable to find an alternative to his leadership, since no Palestinian political system with opposition parties and elections was yet in place. Episodes of violence continue today, resulting in Israeli punitive and security measures, and each such cycle drives angry Palestinians in the direction of Hammas.

Israeli prime minister Itzhak Shamir addressing the Conference of the Presidents of Major American Jewish Organizations in 1987.

"The Handshake." Israeli Prime Minister Yitzhak Rabin shakes hands with Yasir Arafat, Chairman of the Palestine Liberation Organization, with United States president Bill Clinton presiding, September 1993.

The Israeli side also has religious extremists, Jewish fundamentalists who believe that Jews have a divine right to political sovereignty over the entire biblical land of Israel and that they must fight not only the Arabs but also Jews willing to consider yielding sovereignty to anyone else. These extremists are not to be confused with those Israelis who resisted making territorial concessions to the Palestinians for security reasons; most of the latter concede in principle that it would be worthwhile to exchange some part of the conquered territory for a real lasting settlement that would secure Israel from attacks by its neighbors and terrorists. The Jewish extremists are driven less by security than by religious exclusivism, and, like the Islamic fanatics, some are ready to die as martyrs for their beliefs. Many of them are part of the recent immigration of American Orthodox Jews to Israel who have settled on the West Bank,

particularly those who have settled, provocatively, in Hebron.

Negotiations for the eventual complete withdrawal of Israel from the West Bank continue. Arab terrorists have continued attacks on Israeli civilians throughout these negotiations, and Israeli settlers on the West Bank have attempted to expand their settlements, though now against government policy and to the increasing exasperation of much of the Israeli public.

As these lines are being written, the agreement resulting from the second stage of direct negotiations between Israel and the PLO is being signed at the White House. This agreement greatly extends both the territory and scope of Palestinian autonomy. It also provides for elections in Gaza and the West Bank and for the PLO to revise its constitution to eliminate the call for the destruction of Israel, a goal that, as of this writing, the PLO has not formally

Jews in the Twentieth Century: Population Levels by Country and Year

	1939	1949	1959	1995
Argentina	260,000	360,000	400,000	210,000
Australia	23,553	40,000	64,000	91,000
Austria	691,163*	21,500	10,500	7,500
Canada	155,614	185,000	250,000	358,000
Cuba	7,800	10,000	11,000	700
Czechoslovakia	356,830	18,000	18,000	7,600†
France	240,000	235,000	350,000	530,000
Germany	691,163*	55,000	30,000	52,000
Great Britain	300,000	345,000	450,000	296,000
Hungary	444,567	160,000	100,000	55,000
Iraq	90,970	110,000	5,000	100
Mexico	20,000	25,000	25,700	40,700
Netherlands	156,518	28,000	26,000	25,000
North Africa	452,558	400,000	415,000	8,300
Palestine/Israel	399,807	950,000	1,837,000	4,335,200
Persia/Iran	40,000	90,000	80,000	14,500
Poland	3,113,900	80,000	41,000	3,500
Romania	900,000	350,000	220,000	15,500
Soviet Union	4,706,557	2,000,000	2,000,000	817,000‡
South Africa	95,000	N/A	110,000	98,000
United States	4,831,180	5,000,000	5,367,000	5,650,000
Uruguay	12,000	37,000	50,000	23,000

* This is the combined figure for Germany and Austria.

† This is the combined figure for Slovakia and the Czech Republic.

‡ This is the best combined figure available for countries formerly making up the Soviet Union.

renounced. A third stage of negotiations is envisioned that would result in a completely autonomous Palestinian-Arab state in Gaza and the West Bank by the end of the twentieth century. Most Israelis and Jews worldwide are optimistic about the future of the Jewish national home. But no serious observer thinks that the violence is over yet.

As Israel and the Palestinian Arabs come nearer to resolution, the other neighboring Arab countries are gradually also establishing regular relations with Israel. Egypt did so long ago. In September 1994, Morocco became the second Muslim state to establish relations, followed by Tunisia and Jordan. Although Israel and Syria seem to be at loggerheads over the Golan Heights, which Israel won in 1967 and is reluctant to cede in its entirety for security reasons, there is reason to believe that this problem will also soon be dealt with and eventually resolved. Peace with Lebanon, now largely controlled by Syria, could then follow. Even with the Arab suicide bombings of the recent past that have so shaken the Israeli public, the prospect for Israel and the Palestinians' future is more satisfactory now than at any time in the past.

THE DIASPORA

By the time of Israel's independence, the distribution of world Jewry had changed radically. In Europe, only the Jewish communities of England and Switzerland remained intact; on the Continent, the Jews had ceased to be a significant presence, millions having been murdered and millions more having fled. In the Middle East, most Jewish communities were rapidly liquidating themselves, while Israel, though growing, was still rather small, its population growth inhibited first by the British policy of keeping the refugees out, then by the constant warfare and material privation. The Jewish communities of the Western Hemisphere were now dominant. Important Jewish communities had existed in South America (especially in Argentina and Mexico) and

Canada since the turn of the century, and their numbers were now significantly augmented by war refugees. But the Jewish community of the United States was the main center of Jewish population.

For the Diaspora communities, the great question was whether it would be possible to keep Jewish identity and Jewish culture going. For most American Jews, the generation of immigration had become only a fading memory; traditional folkways and beliefs could not withstand the attractions of American society. As time passed, these traditions were associated more and more with aged grandparents and aging parents. Yiddish newspapers and theaters gradually closed; orthodox synagogues were gradually left behind in fading inner cities as America moved to newly built suburbs; and Jewish identity threatened to become irrelevant for multitudes. Even anti-Semitism faded, as third- and fourth-generation Jews grew up with non-Jews, went to school with them, lived side by side with them, increasingly married them, and came to be indistinguishable from other white Americans. Occasional incidents of synagogue desecration were shocking because they were so out of character for America, which had emerged from World War II confirmed in and proud of its commitment to guarantee the freedoms of minorities. Life for Jews in America was so easy that it seemed as if they might merge with the rest of the population and disappear.

The establishment of the State of Israel, though, was an enormous source of pride. American Jewry gave Israel generous financial and political support, both of which were and are indispensable for Israel's survival. But few American Jews went so far as to immigrate to Israel, for there was no incentive to leave America. Indeed, it was only a rare idealist who would consider exchanging the postwar prosperity of America for the material hardship and insecurity of the newborn state.

A pattern of Jewish life emerged in which Jewish identity was expressed through affiliation with a synagogue, mostly Conservative or Reform, and through financial contributions to the network of

Jewish charities and to Israel. Affiliation with a synagogue did not imply a high degree of religious observance, for most congregants were motivated more by group loyalty and ethnic cohesion than by religion. Jewish traditions came to be limited for most people to the observance of the New Year and Passover holidays and to such life-cycle events as circumcisions, weddings, bar mitzvahs (which were increasingly extended to girls and in such cases known as bat mitzvahs), funerals, and annual commemorations of parents' deaths (*yahrzeit*). Few American Jews of the third generation were deeply familiar or truly comfortable with any of these observances.

Jewish identity suffered another blow in the 1960s, with the revolutionary changes brought about by a mass youth culture of political radicalism, sexual freedom, drugs, Eastern religion, and contempt for traditional behavior and authority. In this atmosphere, Jewish behavior suddenly seemed particularly irrelevant to masses of young Jews who otherwise might have continued on the path of gradual acculturation. To this pacifist and officially nonconformist generation, Israel's wars for survival appeared to be the typical actions of yet another militaristic "establishment," and Jewish religious rituals appeared—with some justification—to be just another example of the empty conformism that they attributed to American society in general. Israel, which had been a source of enormous pride to Jews and an object of admiration to liberal intellectuals through the mid-sixties, gradually came to be tarred with the same brush as was being used on the American military-industrial complex. By the time its flower children had come to be of an age to raise their own families, in the 1970s and 1980s, Jewish identity had very little concrete meaning for many of their number.

At the same time, two different kinds of Jewish revival were developing. Among the many thousands swept up by the youth culture were a tiny number who had had a more intensive Jewish education than was usual in the American middle class. This tiny group consisted mostly of young people who had attended educational Jewish summer

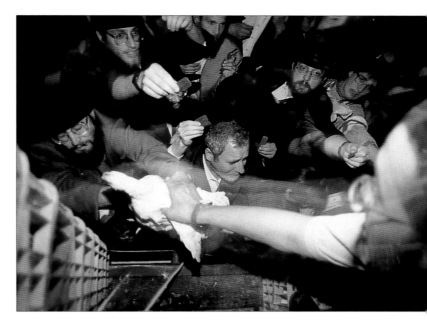

Hasidim crowding around a truck containing thousands of chickens. The chickens are used in a preparatory ritual for Yom Kippur, then slaughtered and eaten.

camps in the late 1950s and early 1960s. In Boston and New York, small groups of Jewish youths arose who synthesized the style and some of the ideology of the youth culture with Jewish traditions. Quite in the spirit of the youth culture, they denounced the Jewish establishment institutions, especially the large, impersonal suburban synagogues and the older generation's unquestioning support of Israeli foreign policy. But unlike their counterparts, these groups were deeply engaged in Jewish affairs, and they were determined to wrest leadership away from an establishment that they saw as less moral and less committed than themselves.

Predictably, the Jewish establishment branded them as destroyers, particularly when they organized demonstrations opposing Israel's occupation of Arab territories in the Six-Day War, thereby openly breaking with the Jewish establishment's tradition of not publicly criticizing Israel. Many supporters of this movement eventually joined the establishment as rabbis and educators, and they introduced a creative—perhaps even spiritual—element into

A Bar Mitzvah being celebrated at the Wailing Wall.

American Jewish education that was not so evident before. They also had a small but significant effect on synagogue life, by encouraging the formation of small fellowships (*havurot*) within large congregations, providing the experience of a more intense Jewish life without the rigidities of orthodoxy.

An unexpected revival of orthodoxy was also arising. Among the refugees at the end of World War II were the remnants of Hasidic groups originating in eastern Europe, some of whom had spent the war years in the Far East, others of whom had survived the concentration camps. These groups joined the Hasidic groups already present in Brooklyn, eventually forming a large and prosperous community. For a long time, they seemed to be merely exotic vestiges of a lost world. Then in the 1970s, one of the groups already established in Brooklyn before the war, the Lubavitch Hasidim, burst into public consciousness under the leadership of Menahem Mendel Schneerson with a dynamic international campaign to win over world Jewry for religious orthodoxy, specifically in the particular form advocated by the Lubavitch.

The Lubavitch campaign, organized with great sophistication and dedication, was surprising in that it made full use of contemporary advertising techniques and technology in propagating a religious style that most American Jews thought of as old-fashioned, even outlandish. Lubavitch missionaries were dispatched to every major population center in the United States and most Jewish population centers worldwide, where they made contact with Jews far removed from tradition and attempted to charm them into simple ritual observances such as lighting candles on Friday nights. The Jewish establishment, which was pouring millions of dollars into trying to solve the problem of reviving Jewish education for the masses of American Jewry, looked on in amazement at the success and influence of the obscurantist rabbi from Brooklyn. Although the actual number of Jews retrieved from assimilation and brought in to the Lubavitch fold was not great, the mere presence of the Lubavitcher Rebbe (as the leader was

Rabbi Menahem Schneerson, the Lubavitcher Rebbe, at a gathering of his followers.

called) in advertisements and on television and the presence of his emissaries in "mitzvah-mobiles" (vans parked in public places blaring traditional Jewish music and manned by rabbinical students trying to identify Jews among the passersby and wheedle them into performing particular religious rites called *mitzvot*) raised consciousness and lent vitality to religious orthodoxy. In the 1980s, the Lubavitch adopted the approach of trying to unite world Jewry in religious observances in preparation for the imminent coming of the Messiah. Rumors soon began to spread that Schneerson himself was the Messiah. Schneerson died in 1994, however, without clarifying the matter.

Lubavitch was not the only evidence of an Orthodox revival. As public consensus on all issues of behavior and morality collapsed in the 1970s and 1980s, many Americans, both Christian and Jewish, began to seek the security of traditional religion. This quest may partly explain the success of Lubavitch, and it certainly explains why many Jews, especially in the New York area, have been drawn to a kind of "modern" orthodoxy. Such *baale teshuva* (repentants) have grown up for the most part in ordinary, suburban, middle-class acculturated homes and have turned to strict religious observance. Unlike the Hasidim, they are full participants in the American middle class, becoming doctors, lawyers, businessmen, accountants, academics, stockbrokers, journalists, and so on. They dress like ordinary middle-class people, for the most part, and participate in the consumer culture typical of American life, but they observe the religious traditions strictly and endeavor to acquire a sound traditional Jewish

education. Now large law firms that before World War II had excluded Jews or limited their numbers have partners who wear traditional head-coverings to work. The trend has been reinforced during the 1980s and 1990s by a general tendency of American society to encourage ethnic differentiation—unlike during the decades immediately following the war, when American society promoted acculturation.

The numbers of these young "modern orthodox" are small within the context of the United States. Some have immigrated to Israel, finding the environment there to be more congenial to leading a totally Jewish life. In Israel, they have tended to identify with the political right, supporting the hard-liners in negotiations with the Arabs; many have even settled in the occupied territories, seeing themselves as a new generation of pioneers who will save "Jewish" territory from falling into the hands of the Arabs. In 1993, to the horror of most Israelis and Jews worldwide, one of their number entered the Cave of the Patriarchs in Hebron, a West Bank town that has not had a significant Jewish population in modern times, and gunned down twenty-nine worshiping Arabs, causing outrage among both Jews and Arabs and creating a major setback in the delicate negotiations between Israel and the PLO then under way.

Although the American Jewish community is the largest outside Israel, there are a number of important Jewish communities outside the United States. It is safe to say that there are Jews in every developed country. Besides those in the Americas, important Jewish communities exist in Australia, South Africa,

TOP: South African Jewish schoolchildren celebrating the release of Anatoly Sharansky from the Soviet Union in 1986.

MIDDLE: Schoolchildren in a *cheder*, a traditional elementary school in the extreme Orthodox community of Jerusalem.

LEFT: Moroccan Jew praying at a rabbi's tomb.

Switzerland (where they were untouched by World War II), and England. On the European continent, France has the largest Jewish community; though their numbers were depleted during the war, they have been replenished by immigrants from Algeria, Tunisia, and Morocco. This immigration has resulted in anti-Semitic outbreaks from time to time.

Surprisingly, a small but well-organized Jewish community has emerged in Germany. Some of its members are Jews who returned after the war; others have come from the United States or Israel in pursuit of business; and still others have emigrated from Russia in search of a better life. The German government has made earnest efforts to protect these small renascent Jewish communities from anti-Semitism, which is still very much alive.

In Poland, which a century ago was the most important center of Jewish life worldwide, there is no longer any significant Jewish population; but there are small organized communities in the Czech Republic and Hungary. Even in Russia, where communism attempted to eliminate all religions and where Jews were actively persecuted at various times under the regime of Joseph Stalin, small Jewish communities have begun to emerge since the dissolution of the Soviet Union. But throughout Europe, and especially in Eastern Europe, intermarriage and assimilation have significantly weakened the Jewish communities that remained after the war.

ABOVE: A Yemenite Jewish woman baking bread.

RIGHT: A Jewish girl from Moshed, Iran.

CONCLUSION:
THE OUTLOOK FOR THE JEWS

In many ways, the Jewish condition in the present is better than it has been at any time since antiquity. The problem of exile, which has defined Jewish history and determined the character of Judaism for centuries, has been solved. In fact, the Jewish problem has found not one, but two solutions.

There is at last a Jewish state. It is again possible, as it has not been since A.D. 70, for a Jew to define his own Jewish identity in terms of citizenship, reducing religion to the status of one among many aspects of the national culture. As an Israeli, a Jew can speak the national language, celebrate the national festivals, live amid the physical remains of the remote Jewish past surrounded by fellow citizens of similar historical background. He can observe the Jewish religious practices if he chooses to, or he can drop them, as have the majority of Israelis.

For Diaspora Jews, it is easier and more acceptable to be a Jewish citizen of a non-Jewish state today than it has ever been in the entire course of Jewish history. Western democracies, especially the United States, guarantee civil rights to all citizens, regardless of their religion. Anti-Semitism has not been eliminated on a popular level, and officials do not always protect the rights of minorities in accordance with the best official principles; but in the western democracies, the Jews are full citizens with full civil rights. In many countries they are well organized and prosperous. Where they have chosen to preserve their traditions and communal structure, they have had little difficulty doing so.

But for Diaspora Jewry, the problem remains that many Jews have not so chosen. Jews fit so well into American society that most have had no trouble merging with it. Judaism in America has always tended to lose its character as a national and historical identity and to identify itself more as a religion. But religion, in turn, receded in importance in American society during much of the twentieth century; as churches emptied out, so did synagogues, until the majority of American Jews had little left of their traditions except for a few food preferences and their last names.

The resurgence of religion in general in America is paralleled by a resurgence of religion among Jews. No one can say where this development will lead. Fifty years ago, it was agreed that orthodoxy could not survive modernity; today it is thriving. It is not that masses of

Jews are joining Orthodox synagogues, but rather that small numbers have become extremely devoted and are raising large families well-educated in Judaism. While it still seems that the vast majority of American Jews are bound to disappear into the general population, as so many already have, it also seems likely that a core will remain passionately attached to the Jewish heritage while living a life very similar in its externals to that of their non-Jewish neighbors.

Fifty years ago, European Jewry had turned to smoke and ashes, and there was no place in the world where the refugees had a guaranteed right to take shelter. American Jewry, for all its numbers, seemed to be poised for assimilation. Jewish identity had little to offer but nostalgia for a dead old world. Today, Israel is a viable Jewish state; it is culturally and intellectually productive, and it is in the process of shaping a new kind of Jewish identity. And America has strong Jewish institutions; Jewish issues regularly attract public attention, and Jewish studies have even found a place in secular universities. Rather than lament our losses and our bitter past, we should be looking forward to the wonderful opportunities that the future is bound to bring.

HISTORY OF THE
JEWISH PEOPLE AT A GLANCE

THE JEWS		GENERAL HISTORY

CHAPTER 1

Patriarchal Period	c. 1900 B.C.	
	c. 1728–1686	Hammurabi king of Babylonia
	c. 1720–1550	Hyksos in Egypt
	c. 1370–c. 1353	Akhenaton Pharoah in Egypt
	c. 1290–94	Ramses II Pharoah in Egypt
Exodus	c. 1280	
	c. 1224–16	Merneptah Pharoah in Egypt
Conquest of Canaan under Joshua	c. 1200	Philistines settle in Palestine
Period of the Judges	c. 1125–1050	
Samuel	c. 1050	
Saul	c. 1020–04	
David	1004–965	
Solomon	965–28	
Divided Kingdom: Rehoboam in Judah, Jeroboam I in Israel	928	
Jehusaphat in Judah	867–46	
Ahab and Jezebel in Israel	871–52	
Athaliah in Judah	842–36	
Jehu in Israel	842–14	
Jeroboam II in Israel	784–48	
Uzziah in Judah	769–33	
Ahaz in Judah	743–27	
Hezekiah in Judah	727–698	
Hoshea in Israel	733–22	
Fall of Israel; exile of ten northern tribes	722	
Sennacherib besieges Jerusalem	701	

Josiah	639–09	Sargon rules Babylonia
Battle of Megiddo	609	
Jehoiachin exiled to Babylonia	597	
Zedekiah	595–86	Nebuchadnezzar rules Babylonia
Fall of Jerusalem; beginning of Babylonian exile	586	

CHAPTER 2

	539	Cyrus takes Babylonia
Beginning of Restoration; first exiles return to Judah	538	
	525	Egypt conquered by Persians
Zerubabel governor of Judah	c. 522	
Second Temple built	520–15	
	465–24	Artaxerxes I
Ezra	458 ?	
Walls of Jerusalem rebuilt under Nehemiah; Ezra proclaims the Torah	445	
	423–04	Darius II
Temple at Elephantine destroyed	411	
	404	Egypt freed
	404–358	Artaxerxes II
	333	Battle of Issus
	332	Alexander the Great conquers Palestine and Egypt
	323	Death of Alexander
	323–285	Ptolemy I in Egypt
	312–280	Seleucus I in Syria
Ptolemy I conquers Palestine	301	
	223–187	Antiochus III in Syria
Antiochus III conquers Palestine	219–17	
Ptolemy IV recovers Palestine	217	
Antiochus III reconquers Palestine	198	
	175–64	Antiochus IV in Syria
Antiochus IV deposes High Priest Onias III	175	
Jerusalem becomes a Greek city, renamed Antiochia	172	
Antiochus IV plunders Temple	169	

The Jews		General History
Antiochus outlaws Judaism, profanes Temple; beginning of Maccabean uprising	167	
Judah Maccabee leads rebellion	166–60	
Judah recaptures Temple	164	
Judah completes conquest of Jerusalem; battle of Nicanor; treaty between Judah and Rome	161	
Judah killed, replaced by Jonathan	160	
Jonathan high priest	152	
Onias IV, former high priest, builds temple in Leontopolis, Egypt	c. 145	
Jonathan killed, replaced by Simeon	142	
Simeon named ethnarch and High Priest	140	
John Hyrcanus High Priest	134–04	
Judah Aristobulus	104–03	
Alexander Yannai	103–76	
Salome Alexandra	76–67	
Pompey intervenes in civil war; Rome takes control of Judea	63	
	44	Assassination of Julius Caesar
Herod is king of the Jews	37–4 B.C.	
	27 B.C.–A.D. 4	Augustus emperor of Rome
Rebuilding of Temple	19	
Pontius Pilate	26–36	
Jesus crucified	c. 30	
Crisis because of Caligula's demand that he be worshiped	37–41	Caligula emperor of Rome
Anti-Jewish riots in Alexandria	38	
Agrippa I	41–4	
	41–54	Claudius emperor of Rome; he issues edict of toleration
	54–68	Nero emperor of Rome
Massacre of Jews of Alexandria; beginning of Judean revolt; Vespasian conquers Galilee	66	
	69–70	Vespasian

The Jews		General History
Ben Ezra synagogue founded in Fustat (Egypt)	882	
Saadia Gaon	882–942	
Death of Hasdai Ibn Shaprut	970	
End of Khazar kingdom	early 1000s	
Death of Samuel the Nagid	1056	
Massacre in Granada	1066	
Jerusalem conquered by Crusaders	1099	
Death of Judah Halevi	1141	
	c. 1145	Almohads in Spain
	1187	Saladin conquers Jerusalem from crusaders
Death of Maimonides	1204	
	1248	Christian conquest of Spain complete except for Granada
	1258	Baghdad conquered by Mongols
Nahmanides in Palestine	1267–70	
	1286	Merinid dynasty of Morocco founded
	1291	Muslims complete expulsion of crusaders

CHAPTER 5

The Jews		General History
	742–814	Charlemagne
Jews begin settling England	1066	William the Conqueror
Crusaders massacre Jews	1096	Beginning of First Crusade in Rhineland
Blood libel in Norwich	1144	
Crusaders again massacre Jews in Rhineland	1147	
Destruction of Jewish community of Blois	1171	
First expulsion from France	1182	
Jews massacred in York	1190	
	1189	Third Crusade
Jews recalled to France	1198	
	1215	Fourth Lateran Council; Magna Carta
Persecutions in western France	1236	

Talmud burned in Paris	1242	
	1252–84	Alphonso the Wise in Spain
Blood libel in Lincoln	1255	
Disputation at Barcelona	1263	
Jews burned at Troyes	1288	
Expulsion from England	1290	
Expulsion from France	1306	
Jews recalled to France	1315	
Expulsion from France	1322	
	1348	Black Death strikes Europe
Jews recalled to France	1359	
Massacres and mass conversion in Spain	1391	
Expulsion from France	1394	
Tortosa disputation	1413–14	
Pope orders censoring of Talmud	1415	
	1431	Burning of Joan of Arc
	1453	Constantinople conquered by Turks
Blood libel of Trent	1475	
	1479	Castile and Aragon united
	1480	Inquisition established in Spain
Expulsion from Spain	1492	Conquest of Granada; Columbus arrives in America
Expulsion from Portugal	1496–97	

CHAPTER 6

Beginning of mass emigration of Spanish Jews to Turkey	1492	
Palestine conquered by Turks	1516	
Joseph Nasi creates duke of Naxos	1566	
Isaac Luria in Safed	1569–72	
Shabbetai Zevi proclaims himself messiah	1665	
	1798–1801	Napoleon occupies Egypt, fails to capture Palestine
	1821	Greek war of independence
	1830	France conquers Morocco

The Jews		General History
Palestine taken by Muhammad Ali of Egypt	1831	
Position of chief rabbi created for Ottoman Empire	1836–37	
Jews granted Turkish citizenship	1839	Westernizing reforms in Turkey
	1854–56	Crimean War between Russia and Turkey, France, and Britain
Damascus Blood Libel	1840	
Alliance Israélite Universelle founded in Paris	1860	
Moses Montefiore visits Morocco	1863	
Jews of Algeria become French citizens	1870	
	1908	Young Turk Revolution
	1914–17	World War I
Salonica fire	1917	
	1932	Iraq becomes independent
	1945	Formation of Arab League
Anti-Jewish violence throughout Middle East	1947	

CHAPTER 7

The Jews		General History
	1510–20	Reuchlin-Pfefferkorn controversy
Ghetto established in Venice	1516	
Inquisition begins in Portugal	1531	
Solomon Molcho burned	1532	
Martin Luther attacks Jews	1544	
	1545–63	Council of Trent begins Counter Reformation
Censorship of Hebrew books begins	1554	
First extant decree of the Council of Four Lands	1580	
	1581	Netherlands becomes independent from Spain
Marranos settle in Amsterdam	1590	
Chmielnicki massacres	1648	
	1649–60	Commonwealth established in England
First Jews arrive in New York	1654	

The Jews		General History
Menasseh Ben Israel in London	1655	
Excommunication of Spinoza	1656	
Death of Baal Sem Tov	1760	
End of Council of Four Lands	1764	
Jews of Eastern Poland under Russian Rule	1772	Partition of Poland
	1776	American Revolution ends with United States independence
	1789	French Revolution
France grants civil rights to Jews; Russia establishes Pale of Jewish Settlement	1791	
Assembly of Jewish Notables	1806	End of Holy Roman Empire
Hamburg Temple opened	1818	
Hep!Hep! riots	1819	
Jews expelled from villages in Russia	1824	
Beginning of large German immigration to U.S.	1836	
Moses Montefiore knighted	1837	
	1848	Year of revolutions in Europe
	1861–65	American Civil War
Ghetto of Rome abolished	1870	
Pogrom in Odessa	1871	
Union of American Hebrew Congregations founded	1873	
Beginning of mass migration to U.S. from Eastern Europe	1881	
Dreyfus Affair begins	1894	
Compulsory military service for Jews of Russia	1842	
Alliance Israélite Universelle founded in Paris	1860	
	1914–18	World War I
	1917	Russian Revolution
Kishinev Pogrom	1903	
Peak of Jewish immigration to U.S.	1906–09	
Beiliss trial in Russia	1911–13	
	1933	Hitler chancellor of Germany
	1939	Beginning of World War II

CHAPTER 8

	1925–27	Hitler's *Mein Kampf* written
	1932	Franklin D. Roosevelt elected president of United States
Boycott against Jews in Germany	1933	Hitler becomes chancellor of Germany
Nuremberg Laws	1935	
Night of Broken Glass; racial legislation in Italy	1938	Annexation of Austria to Germany; Partition of Czechoslovakia
Hungarian Jews lose citizenship; pogroms in Poland	1939	World War II begins with invasion of Poland
	1940	Churchill becomes British Prime Minister
French Vichy regime imposes discriminatory laws against Jews; ghettos in Poland	1940	
Jews prohibited from emigrating from Germany; first death camp established in Chelmno	1941	
	1942	Wannsee Conference
Mass transports to Auschwitz	1942–44	
Danish Jews smuggled to Sweden; Germany declared free of Jews	1943	Germans defeated at Stalingrad and in North Africa; Italy surrenders
Extermination of Hungarian Jewry	1944	Normandy landing
Liberation of concentration camps	1945	Germay surrenders
	1946	Nuremberg trials begin

CHAPTER 9

Moses Hess publishes *Rome and Jerusalem*	1862
Petah Tikva founded	1878
Ben-Yehuda arrives in Palestine; pogroms in southern Russia	1881
Pinsker publishes *Autoemancipation*; Bilu organized; Rishon le-Zion founded	1882
Herzl publishes *Jewish State*	1896
First Zionist Congress	1897

Second Aliya	1902	
Death of Herzl	1904	
Tel Aviv founded	1909	
	1914–17	World War I
	1917	Russian Revolution
British capture Jerusalem	1917	
Third Aliya	1919–23	
British Mandate begins; Arabs riot in Jerusalem	1920	
Herbert Samuel High Commissioner	1920–25	
Weizmann president of Twelfth Zionist Congress	1921	
Churchill White Paper; death of Eliezer Ben-Yehuda	1922	
Fourth Aliya	1924–32	
Hebrew University opened	1925	
Arabs riot in Jerusalem; massacres in Hebron and Safed	1929	
Irgun founded	1931	
Fifth Aliya	1933	Hitler chancellor of Germany
Arab riots	1936	
Peel Commission proposes partition of Palestine	1937	
MacDonald White Paper	1939	
	1939–45	World War II
Death of Jabotinsky	1940	
Palmah organized	1941	
Revisionists strike at British; Jewish Brigade formed	1944	
Intensification of illegal immigration and struggle against British	1945	
Revisionists blow up King David Hotel	1946	
U.N. votes to Partition Palestine	1947	
Israel declares independence; Arab states attack	1948	

CHAPTER 10

First Knesset opens; ceasefire agreements with Arab states; Ben-Gurion prime minister	1949	
Yemenite Jews flown to Israel	1949–50	
Iraqi Jews flown to Israel	1950–51	
Weizmann dies; reparations agreement with Germany	1952	
Moshe Sharett prime minister	1954–55	
Mass immigration from Morocco	1954–55	
Sinai campaign	1956	
Eichmann brought to Israel	1960	
	1964	PLO founded
Six-Day War; unification of Jerusalem	1967	
War of Attrition begins; Golda Meir Prime Minister	1969	
Israeli athletes killed at Munich Olympics	1972	
Yom Kippur War	1974	
Likud replaces Labor as dominant political power; Begin becomes prime minister; Sadat comes to Jerusalem	1977	
Camp David agreement	1978	
	1981	Sadat assassinated
Lebanon War begins	1982	
Begin resigns; Shamir prime minister	1983	
Beginning of intifada	1987	
	1988	King Hussein renounces claim to West Bank; Palestinians declare state
Madrid conference	1991	
Labor returns to power; Rabin prime minister	1992	
Oslo accord; signing of document of intent with PLO	1993	
Peace treaty with Jordan	1994	
Assassination of Rabin; Peres prime minister	1995	
Likud returns to power; Netanyahu prime minister	1996	

BIBLIOGRAPHY

GENERAL

Ben Sasson, H.H., ed. *A History of the Jewish People.* London: Weidenfeld and Nicolson, 1976.

Ben Sasson, H.H., and S. Ettinger, eds. *Jewish Society through the Ages.* London: Vallentine, Mitchell, 1971.

Encyclopaedia Judaica. 16 vols. and supplements. Jerusalem: Keter Publishing House, 1972–1989.

Finkelstein, Louis. *The Jews.* 4th ed. New York: Schocken Books, 1970.

Gribitz, Judah, et al. *Timetables of Jewish History.* New York: Simon & Schuster, 1993.

Schwartz, Leo. *Great Ages and Ideas of the Jewish People.* New York: Random House, 1956.

THE ISRAELITE KINGDOM

Bright, John. *A History of Israel.* 2nd ed. Philadelphia: Westminster Press, 1972.

Shanks, Hershel. *Ancient Israel.* Englewood Cliffs, N.J.: Biblical Archaeology Society, 1988.

THE SECOND JEWISH STATE

Bickerman, Elias J. *From Ezra to the Last of the Maccabees.* New York: Schocken Books, 1962.

Cohen, Shaye J.D. *From the Maccabees to the Mishnah.* Philadelphia: Westminster Press, 1987.

Tcherikover, Victor. *Hellenistic Civilization and the Jews.* Philadelphia: Jewish Publication Society, 1959.

Vermes, Geza. *Dead Sea Scrolls.* New York: Heritage Press, 1967.

THE JEWS IN ROMAN PALESTINE AND SASSANID BABYLONIA

Avi-Yonah, Michael. *The Jews of Palestine.* New York: Schocken Books, 1976.

Neusner, Jacob. *There We Sat Down.* Nashville: Abingdon Press, 1971.

THE JEWS IN THE ISLAMIC WORLD, PART I

Ashtor, Eliahu. *The Jews of Moslem Spain.* 2 vols. Philadelphia: Jewish Publication Society, 1992.

Cohen, Mark R. *Under Crescent & Cross: The Jews in the Middle Ages.* Princeton, N.J.: Princeton University Press, 1994.

Goitein, S.D. *Jews and Arabs: Their Contacts through the Ages.* New York: Schocken, 1974.

Lewis, Bernard. *The Jews of Islam.* Princeton, N.J.: Princeton University Press, 1984.

Stillman, Norman. *The Jews of Arab Lands.* Philadelphia: Jewish Publication Society, 1979.

THE JEWS OF MEDIEVAL CHRISTENDOM

Marcus, Jacob R. *The Jew in the Medieval World.* New York: Meridian Books, 1960.

Parkes, J. *The Conflict of the Church and the Synagogue.* 2nd ed. New York: Hermon Press, 1974.

———. *The Jew in the Medieval Community.* 2nd ed. New York: Hermon Press, 1976.

THE JEWS IN THE ISLAMIC WORLD, PART II

Chouraqui, André N. *Between East and West: A History of the Jews in North Africa.* Philadelphia: Jewish Publication Society, 1968.

Lewis, Bernard. *The Jews of Islam.* Princeton, N.J.: Princeton University Press, 1984.

Stillman, Norman. *The Jews of Arab Lands in Modern Times.* Philadelphia: Jewish Publication Society, 1968.

THE JEWS OF EUROPE AND AMERICA

Mendez-Flohr, Paul, and Jehuda Reinharz. *The Jew in the Modern World: A Documentary History.* New York: Oxford University Press, 1980.

Meyer, Michael. *The Origins of the Modern Jew.* Detroit: Wayne State University Press, 1967.

Roth, Cecil. *A History of the Marranos.* 4th ed. New York: Hermon Press, 1974.

Sachar, Howard M. *The Course of Modern Jewish History.* Cleveland: World Publishing Co., 1958.

Weinryb, B.D. *The Jews of Poland.* Philadelphia: Jewish Publication Society, 1973.

THE DESTRUCTION OF EUROPEAN JEWRY

Dawidowicz, Lucy S. *The War Against the Jews.* 2nd ed. Ardmore, Pa.: Seth Press, 1986.

Hilberg, Raul. *The Destruction of the European Jews.* 3 vols. New York: Holmes & Meier, 1985.

ZIONISM AND THE BIRTH OF THE STATE OF ISRAEL

Hertzberg, Arthur, ed. *The Zionist Idea.* Garden City, N.Y.: Doubleday, 1959.

Laquer, W. *A History of Zionism.* New York: Schocken Press, 1989.

Sachar, Howard M. *A History of Israel from the Rise of Zionism to Our Time.* New York: Alfred A. Knopf, 1979.

JEWISH LIFE AFTER 1948

Heilman, Sam. *Portrait of American Jews: The Last Half of the Twentieth Century.* Seattle: University of Washington Press, 1995.

Sachar, Howard M. *Diaspora: An Inquiry into the Contemporary Jewish World.* New York: Harper and Row, 1985.

———. *A History of Israel, Vol. II: From the Aftermath of the Yom Kippur War.* New York: Oxford University Press, 1987.

Wertheimer, Jack. *A People Divided: Judaism in Contemporary America.* New York: Basic Books, 1993.

PHOTOGRAPHY CREDITS